# SURVIVING OLD AGE

## FROM SLIPPING AWAY TO LIFE AFRESH

MACK TRAVIS

Tadorna Press
ITHACA, NEW YORK

# SURVIVING OLD AGE
## From Slipping Away to Life Afresh

Copyright © 2023 Mack Travis
All rights reserved.
No part of this book may be reproduced
in any form without written permission from the publisher,
with the exception of brief excerpts for review purposes.

Published by Tadorna Press, Ithaca, NY
www.tadornapress.com
ISBN: 978-1-7343229-8-9
Production: Della R. Mancuso
Design: Donna Murphy
Cover illustration: Lynn Keller
Back cover photo: Tony Sorhaindo
First edition

# CONTENTS

. . .

*Compromise*
7

# INTRODUCTION
9

## Part One
## UNDERSTANDING THE LIFE FORCE
11

## Part Two
## SLIPPING AWAY
25

## Part Three
## LIFE AFRESH
85

*Dedicated to our Family, Friends, and Loved Ones.*
*May they come to understand…*

# A COMPROMISE

• • •

My wife, ten years younger than I, said she would refuse to read a book with the title "SLIPPING AWAY." It sounded too threatening, too depressing. But that was the title—that's what I felt was happening to me. Who knew where it was going? I didn't. "Slipping Away" seemed to be a pretty accurate description of my state of mind.

The process of writing this book became an exploration. Life's Force was a given and apparent to me. But after that, who knew where it would lead.

Gradually the stream of consciousness unfolded. It was threatening. It was depressing. But it also grew to become positive—one could survive old age; indeed, one could even thrive in old age.

And hopefully that's where this book takes us, through the obvious limitations of our later years, but with the sheer will, adaptation, friends, memories, loves, and acceptance, perhaps this book will help us realize how we too can thrive in this final phase of our lives. So with hopes Carol will read it, here's the new title: *SURVIVING OLD AGE from Slipping Away to Life Afresh*.

# INTRODUCTION

. . .

Turn off the rational mind for a bit—where will it take you? Out of conscious control—exploring the nooks and crannies of the moment—the unconscious-conscious.

It can be a delightfully uncontrolled journey, if you allow the mind to follow the tangle of threads we typically keep so neatly controlled.

Perhaps Old Age allows one to do that—relax the control. Perhaps in Old Age you have no choice but to relax control. However, it turns out, rest assured it will be different than any mental state you have experienced to date.

What follows is not quite a poem, although at first glance it may appear to have been conceived as a poem. It is the free-associative stream of consciousness—through Covid, through near death—an exploration of memories and solutions—self-generated sheer will, which overcomes slipping away into oblivion and into a realization and exploration of Life Afresh, renewed will, and joy, even as we occasionally slouch and stumble, forget, and experience this new territory of Old Age, as discovered in the nooks and crannies of Unconscious-Consciousness—May you enjoy it!

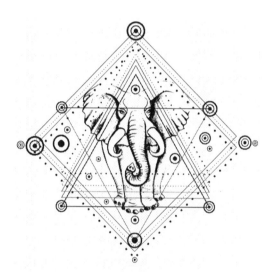

# Part One

◉ ◉ ◉

# UNDERSTANDING THE LIFE FORCE

## Where Did You Begin
• • •

Receiving your mother's first kiss.
Your father's first nuzzle as he
Holds you learning to walk.
As he sets you free for your
First step—on your own.

Where did you begin?
In a passionate embrace
In the Cosmos. And where will
You end? —In a passionate
Embrace in the Cosmos.

And in between?
Your life—your singular life.
As you have been directed
Developed—and chosen
Your own way—utilizing
The Exquisite Energy of
The Life Force.

Desire—from mother's milk
To Pablum and honey.
The urge to pee and poop—
The urge to be clean and in
Control—all desired
All learned—All perfected.
Life's Force—we are designed
To receive it, utilize it,
Even to strengthen it—
In our own way—as we give
Our first kiss, hold another's

Hand and move closer—

Even as we fight and
Scuffle to hold our place in line
And miraculously receive
Encouragement from voices
Around us to step out, finish
What we have begun—
And stand on our own.
We are ready; we are formed—
Like a healthy plant—strong
Blossoming—receiving Life's Force.
And Desire moves us on.
What do I want?…So many
Choices. What do *I* want?

## Silence
• • •

A more open path to
Life's Force. Let it move
Into me—moment by moment.
Silence is the path. In that quiet
Instant of inspiration the idea forms
For the next move—and move we must
Toward nourishment, health, growth
Wanted or unwanted, realized
Or even and often unrealized,
Automatically…We grow.
Life's Force given freely with, even
Without awareness, courses through,
Around, enveloping every cell,
Every thought—exploding instant
By instant through this open chalice

That is us—unless we block it
With our choices turning it into
Anger, blackness, struggle—and it
Shrivels and pauses in the puddle
We become as the chalice empties
And pours out.

Silence is the path that reabsorbs
Our spirit setting us free again
Unblocked, moving quietly toward
Nourishment, health, and growth.
Silence—slipping away to joy,
Bliss, accomplishment.
Pause, be quiet. Listen.

## Expansion
• • •

Accept direction from those
Who know. Listen, learn, repeat
And grow. We quickly learn—
The path reopens to us.

What makes us happy. Radiant
With satisfaction we move
Forward. We expand into life.
Relationships spur us on.
The more we know—the more
We want to know. Let me go.
Let me go. And…
No one is holding us back.
We are thrilled to be moving,
Expanding forward on

Our own. Life's Force flows
Freely through us.
The path is clear. Silence is paying off.

We self-correct with each step.
How old are we? —Old enough
To know, old enough to know
What we want and how to get it.
Silence, inspiration—love
Flow freely through us.

We want what we want.
We will ourselves to it.

## Satisfaction
• • •

Satisfaction leads to more
Satisfaction—it comes to us.

Awareness of the process. Staying
Still, as mind and heart expand, drawing
Us forward—self-correcting, merging
Us with others, growing with them
As we form healthy, fascinating
Charming, and productive relationships.
We work at it. And this work is
A joy, as the energy flows back
And forth, back and forth, thrusting
Us forward into stillness and growth,
Stillness and growth—ever-more
Growth.

Children emerge—

Demanding, reminding us of the
Process—how necessary we are, as
Sharing takes over. It is we who
Are "creating the world" in our
Small way that connects us to
The Cosmos—creating joy, more
And more joy unless we forget,
And block it on a "bad day." A
Kiss, a hug, a word from inside
Guides us back on the path—
Life's Force at work in us—
Through us—continuing the process—
Bursting with joy again and again
Drawing our children and friends,
Our love and lover—singular in
Focus—forward we move.

## Connected
• • •

Why not? Why so? We are
Connected to others. Connected
To ourselves. Fur from our animals
Snuggles softly in our touch—
Windows open. Fresh air
Delights us with energy and
Sunlight. We walk among the
Trees—merging again and again
With each other, our thoughts our
Challenges.

What do we want to do?
The City draws us—the commotion,
The livelihood…Figure this out—

So many have gone before—so many
Are here now! Reaching out. Exploring.
We can do this. Society is a word
We understand. Traffic we know.
Yet we are still—inside.

We needn't be swept away. Turn here
Go there. Shoot forward. Slow down.
There is a pulse here. There is a
Pulse in us. It quickens as we
Adapt. It roars through us—and
We find we are a part of
Everything. Everything is a part of us.

And yet we are still inside.
Stillness is key to the experience.
Joy lies in the stillness, and yes—
In the traffic too.

## Choices
• • •

The choices appear in an endless
Procession. We select. We stumble.
We rise again—thrust forward by
Our own desire—making faces as
We explore—endless procession.

Cracked crystal reminds us, as we
Trace each endless line still contained
In the glass—this hardened chalice
That holds together despite the
Broken lines that intersect—surface
Cracks only—that we are whole,

Intact—it reminds us—we have
Shape, existence, strength and
Beauty—it reminds us.

## Share
• • •

Throw that one away. Find
Perfection as nearly
As possible—return to Silence, which
We know, we experience, we trust
As the Path, as best we can. Breathe
Hard. Breathe rhythmically. Share
Our life, our handshake—our embrace
And smile, as we race ever forward—
Silence at our core. Belatedly we
Remember to tell our story. We
Act it out—for fun—to show friends
And family even a wider audience—

That yes, we are real, whole, happy
And willing to share—Join us. Come
Daily—moment by moment interfacing
Into the metaphor that is us—
Be you with us—you too. Tightly
Wound into our blood and sinew—
Our skin and bone as deeply into
Another as you can go. Take
Us with you in your travels
Sharing your joy as well. I love
You. We can say that—for we
Feel it—I love you. And now we
Know what it means—to stop,
Poise, and be with you and

Within, our spirits together as the
Traffic flows outside, and we
Wonder what to do next.

## Solutions
• • •

Solutions—
Flow forth from the interaction.
Strength overtakes us in a surge
Of activity. Why wait? Do we
Bother? Yes, we bother. It is
All about bothering! Nervously
We eat our lunch wondering
What happened. What will happen…
And Silence is the key.

Tell me what you want.
Tell yourself what you want.
You know. Deeply you know.
In deep you know. Express
It privately to yourself. Tell me what
You know—Do you love me enough.
STOP IT! Swerve and return to me!
We don't want to. We say that to ourselves…

## Exploration
• • •

Traffic turns to Travel. We explore
The local boundaries—explore the edges
Along the sides—we step over—outside
And run through the fields, explore in
The mountains—with friends—with
Ourselves. Creek and gorges. Rough

Water and Kayaks, still water—canoes
Perhaps. Swim through it. Laugh as
The baby fish nibble at our toes.
Kiss me. We're together. Hug me and
We're apart—racing alone. Take
Me with you. No. We'll be alone for a
While. We must be alone. We—
Turns into me.

## Driving and Roles
• • •

Driving fast. Radar protects us—an
Additional "Sixth Sense"—6th Sense—
Warning us of dangers from the outside.
Radar—Radar—some of the dangers as
We drive to fulfill our roles. Do we
Accept them? Mother, wife. Father, husband.
Brother, sister. Uncle, son. Aunt, daughter.
Nephew, niece. Cousin, grand cousin to
Our first cousin's children. Godmother,
God Father. Sister-in-law, Brother-in-law--
Swerve to avoid the
Negativity entering from the right—
The noisy mass of steel thundering
From behind. The roles—our roles—
And that's just our family. They don't
Exhaust us. We belong. They thrill us
And support us.

Keep driving. Carefully
Get there. Carefully navigate into
Their midst. You set out alone—
Or so you thought. And you're never

Alone, free from your roles. They
Hang on you like glue. Like love.
Like hate and trembling? Some do,
But they are your roles. Play them.
And that's just the beginning. We
Return to silence—inside where we
Also live and play a role—the evolving
Role that is us. We're not driving. We're
Just existing—drawing power and
Direction from existence—the goo
That is us—forming it, shaping it with
Attention—or inattention, and it remains.
Just go.

A decision drives it on, forms
It into a shape and gives it direction.
We find it pleasing, and new roles
Present themselves—our roles—
The roles we want. We attach
Them to us before they slip away
Into existence without us. We
Are what we want. Desire thrills us.
Fulfillment and the work that it is—fulfills us.
Life's Force sees to it! Stay open—

# Part Two

⊙ ⊙ ⊙

# SLIPPING AWAY

## The First Crack
• • •

What was their name? It's in here.
Somewhere. The first crack. It's in
There in the first crack—deeply and
The crack widens. S…! Watch your
Language. There are children present.
You return from this minor abyss—
Jim?…John?…You pretend for a moment—
Smiling. Someone calls out to them by
Name—and there you have it. You
Relax…Of course. You did know it—
All along, you tell yourself. It's
Okay now. Relax. Continue the
Conversation. You don't need names to
Converse—just smiles and content.
You still have content. It is all OK.

## What's Ahead
• • •

Dizzy? You stumble just a bit—
That first misstep. No one notices.
It's OK. You're all right. A deep breath—
There's silence in there. You're perfect
In silence, and you can always return.
You slip away outside—fresh air—
And stop using that term—you're OK.

It's like solving that first math problem
At your desk. You got some help and
It's all right to get help—you can see
Better into the future—what's ahead.
More problems? You can always

Get help. You'll get a good grade—

That's important—to get a good grade.
But. But…No—you can do it. In
Silence, you can do it. You can always
Smile—always return to Silence.
Excuse yourself for a moment, and
Slip—SLIP—No. No. It's in there
Somewhere. No more slipping—not now.
Not until next time… And there will always
Be a next time---always be a next
Time—always—Until there isn't.

## The First Episode
• • •

Is that a flea biting me? Reach
Down. You have dogs. It may well be
A Flea—scratch—uh—it's not polite to
Scratch. People will notice. Suppress the
Urge…to scratch. Go outside…no one
Will notice. Scratch all you want. Could
This just be dry skin? And don't spit.
Or clear your throat so loud and
Noticeable. Stay outside for a bit. It's
Private in the outdoors. You're part of
Nature—after all—you're part of
Nature. Nature and all its cycles.
They are a part of you. The family will
Not miss you. Colleagues--? No one
Not for a while. You forgot, stumbled,
Scratched, and spit—the First Episode.

There are creams and drops. Vitamins

And supplements—one by one you add them
And they contribute to normality.
If you focus on something—that's
What you'll get. Sleep. It feels good.
You needn't always be in motion—
Acting—with your lists—your tasks.
But if you're not acting, accomplishing—
Are you really alive? Really? Will
You become all you can be—all you
Envision. Before it's too late. It's not too late!
You can explore. At your own pace.

## Turn Inward
• • •

Turn inward to Silence. You can explore
Silence—just as you have explored the
World—the trips—the cultures—the
Rivers—the people—strange, new, imposing
Themselves on your sensibilities, because
You came for this, you let it happen.
You have values. You have limits. You
Can draw the line. Even if it's only next
Door, or within the family—you can,
And choose. You don't need every experience.

Choice is always an option—in your
Control. But it's the trips that are
So glorious expanding sensibilities—
World-wide into change and difference.

## The Bonds
• • •

What is it you seek? Together—to be

Together—and the strangeness—the newness
Forms as a bond between you—you
And you and you—your traveling
Companion(s)—for life.
It's almost too good
To be true. But it is true—the bonds
Between you—forming—releasing—
And on to the next place, the next
Experience—Even to come back—to
Return—revisit. It's healthy. The
Memories are solid. They do not fade—
Even in the pictures. They will always
Be with you—sharing the bond as
Though you are in love—and you are!
In love—Nourished and filled with joy.

And you can go back. You can always
Go back—Until you can't. The world
Erupted there. So and so is gone. So and
So is dead—Imprisoned. It's so rough
And unfair. Not everyone shares
Your sense of loss. The world is a strange
Place. What's their name? Where
Was that? I used to know. Do you
Know? Do you remember? Take me
Back with you. You can't?...

Hold my Hand… Please.
That's better…I remember
Your touch—the searing joy of being
With you. Wait! Who are you? Was
That you? You assure me that it is—
You. Silence returns. Life's Force

Is active—but it does seem to change.
It can't change. But something is changing.
Never mind. What was his name? If you
Focus on something that's what you'll get,
And you remember.

## Heart to Heart
• • •

It's not necessary. The mingling of our
Private Parts. Mingling. There's joy
In mingling. There's capability in mingling—
Until there's not. Not. Not necessary—
Heart to Heart—we pound our way
Through to a glory few know—Do we
Know? We're given a path. Many are
Given a path. You can be confident—you
Can join this Silence—roaring through
Space to infinity—Infinity among the
Gods. The GODS? Can it be? We study
History—the History, our history—it's
Inside—Heart to Heart. Soul to private
Soul. Remembering is not necessary here.
Slamming against the unopened door is not
Necessary here. Quiet assuming. Quiet knowing.

## Oozing Joy
• • •

Occasional peaks of spirit—sailing is
A silent thing. Between us. Between
Us and the Ocean. We're together—outside
Of memory—doing—doing—Peaks of spirit as
We give it all away to others—to those
Coming along—on the path—oozing joy.

It's not to be helped oozing joy. Why stop—
It comes naturally. Silence contains the transaction
As you smile, kiss, and blow yourself
Away—on the wind to parts and places
Heretofore unknown to you—to them—to
All who connect, touch, speak, and smile
In your ever-growing circle of Transaction.

## Feeling Broken
• • •

Leave me out of this. Feeling broken
Today? There are things to do. Important
And necessary. Oh?... They are on my
List. Here, see! On my list. You're
Too old. Who says that? It's on my
List. Grounded. Remembering. Important.
Too old is not an option. Open up.
Forget what you forgot. This is spirit here.
Spirit! Silence…gods…in there somewhere
Who knows? You know. Shine. Ooze—
Beat me down…To memory—little shards
Of memory—a simple place bordering on
Silence. Life rumbling around. Life's
Force returning. Take me with you.
Heart to—you are so necessary to me—
Heart. Tell me where we're going. You
Seem to know. Certainty reassures me.
Thank you. Here's my list for today.
Put it away. Take it as it comes—for today.
We're going together. Family, friends.
You can say it. Thanks… Giving…
Oh yes. It all makes sense. It's
Why we're here. Today—No list. Giving—

Remember. No list. Let it be. There's so
Little time. Thanks. We can do it. You
Know we can do it. And it's so necessary.
Together.

## Wisdom
• • •

Wisdom—independent of stumbling.
Surpassing dizziness and imperfection.
Existing in the overall realm of
Completeness that is you—us, channeling
Energy and analysis of content and
Details provided by another needing help
Or advice in how they fit together.
The experience of years—you've been
Here before—on the path—figuring
Out for yourself—moment by moment—
Twist by turn, always flexible existing
Alongside you—permeating thought
And action. You've given Thanks—It's
Time to share. Vitality. It restores you
To pass it on. Throwing out the chaff absorbing
It all—getting to the heart of the matter.

Here's what to do—if you go this way, that
Will happen. If you go that way—this
Will Happen. You ask your friend, your
Lover, your protégé—what do you want to
Happen? Listening, simply, shifting thought—
Wisdom is not judging—not in the sense of
You are bad for even thinking this.
Wisdom is independent of all that, and at a
Deeper more basic level—it is the ability

From having had results based on this
Or that action yourself, to be able to tell
Another what to expect—what actions to
Consider that will likely give them
The results they want.

This growing older has its benefits, as you watch
The one who has come to you for answers,
Advice and direction, and they fly
Forward with energy and thought—
Processes you had assisted them in
Directing—and Yes! They make the deal—
Shape the relationship—invent and
Follow their own path using those
Principles of Nature you—in your
Wisdom—you pass on to them—as they—
If you think back—and you always
Think back—giving Thanks to those
Who once and so many times throughout
Your life—passed on to you. It works
That way. The basics—to the Stars—
It's all there for you to—pass on
The confluence of Energy—Universal
The recognition of receptivity, creativity
In an individual or group and the
Conviction that you have the duty—
And the delight to speak up. You are
Not shy. Wisdom unfolds the
Interaction that creates the successful outcome
They desire. Mentoring—independent of
Dizziness and Stumbling—pure clear thought.
Wisdom has developed in you, and you pass it on.

## Fog
· · ·

Where's the light house through the fog?
It's on the chart. We're close. Fog.
Mold—it's in the basement. I'm
Totally lost. Not perceiving—or thinking
Clearly—just reacting—Fearful—yes
Fearful. You've been here before.
It's not dark—just foggy. Moldy.
You're checking—having it checked. You
Read—Spores—produce, or can, dizziness,
Loss of short-term memory. Shortness of
Breath—could it be pneumonia—just
Fog? Not you. You're not wise—
Just doing what you can to remember to
Hold direction—Worried? —Yes a little—
Will outcomes be rocky—stay offshore
Sleep. When you can. Sleep. Forget…

## Cycles
· · ·

Routine. Cycles. Every day has its cycles.
Every heartbeat has its cycle. Every
Breath. Every touch. Every fork full is
Swallowed. Every step is taken and
Taken, and taken. Go out. Come in. Sit
Down, get up. Feel good about yourself—
Feel not so good. Expansion, Contraction.
Purpose moves us forward. No purpose—
Routine takes over. Silence keeps us in
The Current—bouncing along shore to
Shore—raging, still, cataracts, and eddies.
Life Force carries us downstream. Routine…

Routine—keeps us afloat. Dark days, foggy
Days—Brilliant sunshine, pouring rain—
Routine keeps us afloat in the current.

## Routine
• • •

Be grateful for it. Fall back on it
Like a reliable life raft supporting us
In the current. We bump the boulders
Still afloat. Today's final cataract dumps
Us ashore, and we pause, dry out and
Regroup bent on finding that path
We were on. Routine has served us for now.

Purpose, Expansion, Happiness—desire for
More, place us firmly back on the path
We have been on for most of our life.
It's there. The path itself is reliable,
Where it is taking us moves us across
Borders into the unknown, unexplored
Fascinating and secure because it is
The path. Silence moment to moment
Points the way. Intuition opens new
Vistas inaccessible in that snarled
Memory we have clung to—unreliable
As it has often become. Never mind.
Use what we can and continue moving
Forward on the path. Our loved ones
Can fill in the gaps, hopefully with
Compassion, hopefully without sarcasm
And the "I've told you this a million times!"

## Comfort
• • •

It's our animals that comfort us—
Little bundles of fur and affection
That bring us joy—Simple flash of
Feathers and a song—a squawk—feed me.
He weighs 160 lbs.—he's only three.
She just had a litter of eight—Eyes
Not even open yet. See how she licks
Them into life. Our parents did the
Same for us—Suckled and nourished
Life Force into our being and through
Us to the world—for a little while.

## On Lock Down
• • •

She was only 23 when she died in childbirth.
He was 36—hit by a truck right on that
Corner—there. My friend was 82 when
He had a stroke. I drove him to Physical
Therapy for two years. He recovered his
Speech. That one over there is 97—and
Down the hall curled into a ball 104—she
Can still open her eyes and say hello.

Your father was in here too—on lock down.
We took his dog for him to see
Through the glass doors. Until COVID
Took him down. In NYC they loaded
Strays into steel cages and drowned them
In the East River. It was in the history book.

## Credit
• • •

Are we crammed into a cage? The TV
Tells us we are free—free to buy anything
We want—and on credit if necessary.
We don't need Wisdom and Revelation—
We just need a credit card. Some go to
Church to break that cycle—to gain
Even more credit to live on. It helps.

## A One or A Thing
• • •

And our animals give us affection.
And when someone or some thing
Dies it leaves a snarled mess—is an
Animal a "one," or a "thing?" He felt
Like a "one"—even through the glass.
And she was a "one" and I held her in
My arms—everyday sometimes close—
Sometimes perfunctory, until he, she,
One—died—but never a thing, and it
Left a snarled mess of emotion until
You remember the cycle and the
Ashes went into the ground, or you
Spread them on the waves in the lake.
It wasn't disrespectful. It was part
Of the cycle. And you were OK.

## Hold Me
• • •

Just hold me in your arms and comfort me—
Despite the fact my fur is coming out—
My skin is wrinkled my memory is fading—

Hold me—please. Comfort me—pet me.
Teeth are not an issue. They only cause
Pain anyway. Hair, fur, memory—
Who needs it—One thing—in your
Arms—everything becomes a One—
In your arms. Just hold me. I love you so.

## Purpose
. . .

Stiffen up. It's purpose that drives you.
No purpose—no drive—just lie there—or
That's the way it's always been. Just be
There, or here. Be here—now. We've
Heard that. How does that relate to us?
Plan ahead—not necessary. Be here.
But plan…No plan. Be here. No plan.
No purpose. Do we descend into existence—
Or rise into existence. False question.

## Meditation
. . .

Don't ask a question—just stop—
Experience—live in it. Rising, falling,
Breathing in, breathing out—slowing
Down—here—Sit down. Use this word—
A meaningless sound. Close your eyes…
Repeat it in Silence—Repeat it again
And again. Silently—ever quieter.
The world outside your eyelids quiets, and
It too "disappears."—No plan. No purpose.
Just yourself—and it opens up—the Space
The Silence—it emerges into the Magnificent
Now—sweeping—the You with it. The You

And the One—no plan, no purpose—just
Existing. You sense Existing. Not old. Not
Dependent. Just being there in the Now
That surrounds you—the NOW that is part
Of your every fiber. Nourishing. Strengthening.
Quieting. For a while. Don't worry about it—
Taking it with you. Just know that you can return
Daily—morning and evening you can
Safely return. In between, the clinging
To purpose and drive become secondary—
Not secondary, but balanced with what
You are "Supposed to do"—You still must
Care for yourself. Care for others.

## The Musts
• • •

Stay open, and the Musts that
Must be done to, quiet to a murmur
And you just do them. It becomes
Apparent what they are—no snarl—
No struggle—taking them one by one,
Or in a heap—however they come to
You. You haven't given up. You
Haven't crawled under a rock—you
Have experienced the depth of no
Experience—the quiet at your core.
It's there—You grow more and
More confident of it as morning
And evening you return—expanding
Into this space that is you—
This "Magnificent Now." So readily
And easily accessible, as you sit
Quietly, close your eyes and repeat

The meaningless sound that takes you deep
Into lack of infirmity, rejuvenating
You. You are not a Thing that can be
Broken—You are a One—that can handle
The "MUSTS" until your very last breath!
You can. And you do.

## Mold
• • •

There's an effort associated with the mold
In your basement—tested—now verified.
A private damp haven where COVID
Drove you a year ago—could it have
Been? It's finished, attractive, with filtered
Air—and it's moldy. For a year—at first with
An oxygen pump for pneumonia—
With the cats—too restless for the house—
For nightly companionship—your buddies—
Your furry companions whose nightly
Inclination to snuggle—fur to fur—
Fur to sheets and skin. Respiratory limitation—
Read about it—loss of memory, dizziness,
The fog as you stumble a bit and catch
Yourself. Math in your head—forget it. Use
The Calculator—and then do it three times to
Check. And that cough—and all that comes
Up with it. The rash—it's disgusting—
But you're old. You "forgot, stumbled,
Scratched and spit"—you're Old—Slipping
Away. Life's Force sucked up in the
Medications. And do you believe it? —

## Self Harm
• • •

The respiratory medicine cost $1.81—One
Dollar and eighty-one cents—the doctor prescribed
It—30 pills—The warning on the paper
They always give you— "May cause suicidal
Thoughts or the urge to self-harm—" If it
Cost $700 you might take it seriously—
One hundred eighty-one cents—that's not
Going in my body—and you can't even
Throw it away… "Dispose of properly"—

You've done it to yourself. There's no
One to blame—It's the cycle. Avoidable
By will? By chance? You doubt it.
Until you read the mold test. It's
Too simple. It's damp. Spore counts
In some cases "off the charts"—
Coughing, dizziness, shortness of breath—
The mental fog—attributable to mold?

## Recovery
• • •

Bring in the Specialists. Move upstairs
To the clean country air by the lake
Where you live. Already, after one night
You feel hopeful. Where you live. How you
Live—no suicidal medicines for you.
Recover fully, as you breathe deep
Healthy breaths in the NOW of
Clean, healthy air. Thank those who suggested
Air tests. Grateful has hardly been in
Your vocabulary—self-centered—

Hoping, clinging to what you were.
There's freedom in renewed hope.

## Purge
• • •

Savor it. Clean the basement. Purge it
Of mold. Purge yourself of worry and
Old age. There's still time. Face it.
Enjoy it. Bring those you love with you.

Unbelievable—as energy flows back into your
System, as clouds lift, thought clarifies and
Expresses. You're steadier without the stumble,
Without the dizziness. It's true. It's been
Foretold—it's the mold. It can't be good for
The cats either. Bring them up into the
Light. A week or two—perhaps the cough will
Be gone. Old age—it will all go in the
Dumpster—a new renewal—trust it and see.

## Gratitude Supports Fortitude
• • •

Fortitude has taken us all far. We gain it from
Each other—we manufacture it for ourselves—
To move—to plan—to give and take. To Be—
Trust it and give Thanks—Gratitude supports
Fortitude. Old slips past us, as we love again—
Ourselves again. We find it in there
Somewhere—where it's always been—
Latent, hidden in infirmity—rolling forth
Now in vitality—Life's Force. Where
Will you go now? A trip—a curative
Trip—with—to—those you love—to see to

Enjoy—more humble now. More fun to be
With. You always speak your mind, although
Sometimes silently. You're wiser now and
Sometimes wise keeps silent. It's the youth—
They are the ones who have the energy. You
Enjoy watching—participating when they
Invite you into the world you created
For them—as was done—yes—for you and you
Will leave it to them—Will—Will power
Will continue to thrive through them as
It has done through you. You will depart
At some point—just not now. And with
As much dignity as you can muster. Mold
Is gone, but they're still there these little blips
On your body, and your hip hurts.

## Walking Sticks
• • •

Enjoy the walk anyway. The dogs expect
It. The walking sticks support you. Only
Old people use those—you told your
Young Austrian guide when he proposed
Them to you for your day's trek to
Torres del Paine in Chile—No, all ages
Use them. Try them, he said. And since
Then, you've used them—trekking in the
Rockies—hiking in the Adirondacks—Like
Ski poles—cross country on the Vasa
Lopet in Sweden—and they work in your
Woods with the dogs. It's only a slight limp
And it really doesn't hurt—much. And
That was long ago. You never stop
Learning until the day you—never stop.

## Remember
• • •

Four things to remember. Eat, sleep,
Exercise, and be merry—merriment
And joy. Talk, spread it around.
Take that curative trip with the one—one—you
Love—to the grocery store, the post office—
To the big city, to the big country—to the world!

## Identity
• • •

Identity—you've left the known so many
Times—the people—the house, the office, the
Job, and finally you created the job. It
Creates you. You create it and then for whatever
Reason—you leave always in the moment for
The new. Life's cycles, the routine is never
Routine, it's supported by every moment's change
And you accept that. Your identity is not
The job—to what are you clinging—the books
The notebooks—50 or more years of diaries,
Journals for work, the books that have
Shaped you—all your life—You want others
To know—a bit of vanity—but maybe there
Is usefulness in all of this. It's you
After all. And it's covered with mold—
But it's you—and yet you know it's not
You—You are energy—thought—ideas—
Not notebooks and archives—yet will they
Not find it interesting—fascinating even. No—
They are covered with mold—Clean them!
Page by page—the specialist asks—Is it
Worth it? You ask—is it worth it? You've

Left a few objective things—written out,
Viable. Does anyone care about the
Dirty laundry that got you where you
Are—or the brilliance of analysis that
Produced the you that still exists—

## Adapt
• • •

Moldy? The spores grow. They wreck your
Stuff—They wreck your brain. Start fresh.
It's apparent moment—by moment what
To do. One hundred miles offshore
The storm is coming. You're in it and
Prepared. Never do you curl up and cry—
NEVER!!! –You ride it out. That's the key.
Every time there is change you adapt.
There is change—or you make the change
Happen. And then adapt. Change flies at
You—you adapt. The energy is fun!
It's not moldy. Not yet. The energy
Within the change. And it's tied up
In the books. Tied up in the files—
The journals—the diaries. They are moldy.

## Hold On
• • •

You are not moldy—You've moved out.
You brought energy with you and
It's quickly restoring—even in old age
It's restoring. Clean the books. Pack
Them away. They can exist outside
The negative energy. There are so many
Ways to go—Exploring—you're not

Through yet. Smile, loosen up. Tell
The man. Tell the woman. Tell the
Child—you love them. Shower them
With gifts—of light, energy, and
Compassion. What you give comes
Roaring back to you. Life Force always
Survives—Latch on. Hold on. Enjoy that trip.

## Forgot
• • •

Even still you forget. That water bottle you
Keep beside you. You take the cool drink
Early in the morning. It's dark. You
Place it beside you in the bed. Snug and
Ready for the next time. The first move
And it spills across the sheet. You forgot
To reaffix the top. It gurgles as you
Quickly upright the bottle and dig for
The top. How could you…

At seven years old—
You overnighted at Auntie's house. You
Wet the bed and in a panic neatly made it
Up without a wrinkle—but then she
Knew. It's all right honey. Better to tell me
And let me help you. The puddle was still there.
Mortified, you helped her change the sheets.
She gave you a hug and fed you breakfast.
You remember that. You forgot the top.

## Love Him
• • •

Sixty years later the phone rings. It's dark.

He hit me again with his back scratcher.
It's the nurse. Your friend at the nursing home
Out of his mind with anger and impotence
Overcome by Oxycodone, grabbed, reached, hit
Even with his stroke—One more incident and
We're strapping him down. You reassure
Her. Did he hurt you? No, but he could have.
You'll come in the morning—
Get him home care. He remembers home.
He just wants to go home. Love him. Someone
Has to love him. Is this what it's coming to?
It was only a top—mop it up. Move on.

You're recovering—out of the mold now.
You will need help. It's there. Accept it.
When you need it. You have friends—
You have family. The circle is growing
Smaller. But it's there. Where will you go next?

## Memory
• • •

Are these trips meaningless? No more meaningless
Than a caress —which is never meaningless.
It stirs the senses. Focuses feeling.
We think more clearly after a caress.
We know who we are, and it feels
Good. A walk in the woods will do, but a
Trip—a trip is colossal! The grocery
Store. The post office… China—energy
Surges through you as you round the next
Corner together with the someone you love—
Or even alone—a curative trip emboldens
You. You don't need a back scratcher—

Not yet. The cycle. The routine. The
Next bend in the river—you can
Count on. The food is good here too.
Sensation defies forgetfulness. Touch.
Sight. Taste. Smell. Thoughts. Lots of
Thoughts. Memory. We've been here before.
But that's a different leaf falling—a different
Squirrel crossing the road. But surely we've
Been here before—It was only a top…

## Compassion
• • •

Rest assured it will have been worth the
Wait, as we move forward. Today is not
The day. We're off course. Churning. Thoughts.
Violence. What's happened? We're peaceful.
We don't strike out. We smile and enjoy
The trip. But today we're not so sure. That's
Normal—Up down. At least were here and
Moving, albeit slowly. Compassion. We
Know what's it's like to care for someone and
Watch as they slip away. He was a wise man.
What's it like? You watch and wait. Where
Do you go, you ask? Nothingness. Cease to exist.
That's all. It's over for what has been you—
But it's not—all those whose lives you
Touched… Nothing. It's over. But it's not.
I will always remember you. But you'll be
Gone—and those after you will be gone—
Gone—Nothingness. Half the world believes
This. It's only an idea. Call me back when
You're feeling better. Life's Force subsumes us.

## The Dreams
• • •

Running down embankments, strange
Cities, cramped back rooms, not so
Friendly people, strange powers wading through
The muck. It's not you. It's weird. You're
Lost, but you're on your way. It doesn't
Feel like a dream—until you awake with
A start as some insurmountable object
Blocks your way. They keep coming—these
Dreams that have nothing to do with your
Reality—Youth in action. Youth fearless
As you remember—traveling alone through
Forests, mountain tops, ferries, and
Seashore. New people—cultures—language.
Take me home with you? Yes, that's
OK. I'm a stranger here—and fearless.

## The Chemicals
• • •

Could it be the chemicals—the old age
Chemicals, for memory, for this infirmity,
That infirmity—the $1.81 suicide decongestant
That you didn't take, or the Arctic Charr—
The newspaper prescribed them. They
Were a good deal. They forgot to mention
The explosive dreams they induce, or
Was it the pasta—the spice—or perhaps
Your inhibited thirst for adventure
As you explore into the cracks of what
You thought—dreamed—is your reality—

## Companionship
• • •

It feels good—a bit jarring—but oxygen
Level is OK. Heart rate—check. It was
Excitement—thrilling—on the edge you have
Faced and lived all your life—on the
Edge—but it was a dream—weird—
Fulfilling in a bizarre way. Maybe
You should drop the pills—stick with the
Aspirin, reduce the ten combinations—
Or is it twelve, or fourteen you ingest every day?
Balance out through for forgetfulness and
Bad dreams. They weren't "bad"—just
Stretching relationships and situations
To the limit—as you have always done—
Hug your significant other"—the spouse
Who crawls into bed next to you with
Their own bad dreams. Companionship is
A cure in itself. The soft caress and
The smoothness of whispered words in the
Dark. It's always been that way—
Even in violence, breakdown and
Betrayal—we're human after all—only
Human. Maybe bad dreams help keep
Us on the path—not likely—sunlight
Is a better cure. Sweet words off the
Page that delight us and take us to
Safety and security as we imagine our
Own exploits. Those days are over. No!

## Hold On
• • •

Hold on. Moment to moment is still within our

Purview. It can always be our reality.
There's safety in it. Adventure too. Life
Force doesn't stop—breath to breath—heart to
Heart. It's fabulous. Always has been.
Hold the little child. Hold the adolescent—
The thriving middle-aged success. They're
All going through it—and share their strength.
It's beautiful—breathing in—breathing out.
Maybe those memory pills work after all—

# Friendship
• • •

For over 40 years we've been best of
Friends—40 years—well 42 to be exact.
And every year your birthday slides by
Unremembered. Is it the 2nd or the 10th?
You live half a country away now.
Embarrassment prohibits calling any more—
It's probably the 2nd and by the
10th it's too late to send a card—
Another year forgotten. You're not
Forgotten. Friendship claws at us over
The miles, over the years. Maybe in the
Summer we'll meet at the coast—sail
Together in the swells and forget we
Forgot, in the joy of the salt spray that
Pries and pinches us into the moment,
And the moment fills our senses at sea.
Another birthday looms—mine, and you
Always remember. Embarrassment is small-
Minded. Half a year away. Hardly worth
Bringing up. Not worth bringing up. Don't
Go there. Not needed in the salt spray

Of the sea. And we shoot forward in
The swells. Who's smarter? Who's
Achieved more in their life. Are we
Not friends—without question. Self-
Reinforcing one another for 4 decades.
Sailing in the swells. On this strong boat
Of Friendship that takes us wherever we desire
To go—rough or calm—it makes no difference
Moment by moment. Maybe next year I'll remember.

## The Edifice
· · ·

Tomorrow has come.
Don't count on me. Drifting away—
In dreams of Egypt—missing the
Promises made to be there—do that—
It's all in a fog. Never good enough—
You've worked all your life to overcome
That—shriveled it up in a vague memory
That creeps out now and then and today
Overcame the lists, the reliability that
Has been your strong suit—built this
Edifice that is you and is slipping away
Around you. It's the people that propped
You up, and they are leaving, driving down
The road—one by one. And it's the youth
That still see the edifice—strong—strong? —
Oh, it's crumbling a little. Day by day. Meeting
By meeting. Lunch by lunch., By dinner
It will be in a heap—probably—likely.

## Deflated
• • •

Maybe they'll return on time—to remind
You. It's only a glass door—You're fine
And we see you—here have some dinner.
And you're not fine. You feel totally deflated.
Where are those pills? Take more of them.
Take a handful—No! Don't. Don't. Don't.
Do not! It's too late to make amends
That need to be made. They're wheeling you
Out on a gurney—or is it a walker—
Or maybe just a cane. Totally deflated—You
Forgot and let them down. It's all
Out there—the walker, the cane, whatever
You need for support.

## The Patches
• • •

You cannot be yourself in the mess. The
Friends, the sons, the daughters—the
Significant—dog—who remembers
You and licks your hand. The other is
Out shopping—for you—for your
Dinner—and you can be there, or you
Can be in a fog. Your choice. Get it
Together. Sorry isn't good enough. You
Need a steady stream of consciousness
That's in there somewhere. Be still.
Draw on it. Draw yourself through
It. You've been here before. It will pass.
Take it one thing at a time—the scabs—
The teeth—the dry and wrinkled skin—
It will not pass. You're here now in

This moment. You're a little damp. It's
The humidity. Not it's not… Oh, my God.
Get used to it. The edifice is there to
To remember—when you can. Others
Can. It's a sunny day. You can see
Clearly—the patches you've put on
To hold yourself together. And it's all right.
Everyone has a few of them. Smile back.

## Obsessions
• • •

Hold onto your list with an iron fist—as you
Have all your adult life—journals, diaries,
Daily accounting—work notes—shelves and
Shelves of them. An obsession—probably is, but
Such a tool they have been—why give up now?
Memory books to jar you into reliability—
Reality as other people see it—the normal
People. It's fine. Little did you realize
How effective they have been. Don't stop now.
Pills, memory books, walks with walking sticks—
It's safer. Smile. Talk, but not too much—
To yourself. It's pleasant. You know a lot.
It's OK, to keep yourself oriented. Talk to
Yourself, but remember the others—they expect
To hear from you when you're present.
It's nice—awfully nice in here—these four
Walls of your head. There's not so far to slip…
Aah—open your mouth and hope something
Comes out. It seems so worthwhile in
Your head. If you could talk, it would
Be even better. Stay on schedule. Check your list!

## Doggie Gibberish
• • •
Talk to the dogs—in a heap around you.
They understand whatever you want to
Tell them—even doggie gibberish—it's the
Tone—all in the tone and the strokes through
Their soft brown fur. You saw a puppy
Yesterday—Tucker—New brown life to touch
And rub. Never be afraid to expect the
Best…. the neighbors don't need to know.

## Time Warp
• • •
Only your family and close friends
See the tremble. The stumble is more
Difficult to hide. Take that curative
Trip. You can still drive. They haven't
Taken away the keys yet. The radar
Detector is such a boon—keeps you safe
At high speeds—secure in your cocoon.
It saves you money, as you enjoy the
Thrill again of 20, 30, 40, and now you're
Nearing 90, not quite—the piercing flash
Of danger hasn't gone off yet. You might
Even reach 100. It's a time warp, this
Speed and age—which is it? As the
Deer amble out in your head lights, is it
Age or speed? You swerve and don't care.
You can be 100 doing 100, or 70 doing 70.

At 16 you obeyed the rules. They gave
You the keys. You learned to stretch the
Boundaries. You broke the boundaries.

You were a success, and now you're on
Your curative trip—you can reach 100,
But you can't be 70 again. This used to be
A new car. The shimmy started about 70. Push
It anyway to 100. The piercing flash may be
The red lights of the radar detector protecting
You, or the ambulance coming to get you. But
This is your curative trip, and you don't care.

## Caring
• • •

This morning you woke up with no will—
Too many choices—none of which you
Want to choose. But you must. So many
Rely on you—count on you—need you—
But now they don't. The youth are launched.
There is no one—nothing out there on
Which you need to make a difference.
This is an illusion—a bad dream—only
It isn't. You forgot—to take your pills
Yesterday. Could that be it? Someone
Cares. You took them to lunch yesterday.
They told you…They looked fine…They
Looked normal—but they told you, they
Can't remember ANYTHING! They don't go
Out. Thank God for caregivers. They don't
DO ANYTHING—but they looked normal.
You hugged and smiled and cared for
Them, and that was enough. You felt
Useful. You talked normally. You paid
The bill. And caring was enough.
Enough for both of you and your
Friends who were along. It all appeared

Normal. You talked of the children—
Their accomplishments—the 50+ year
Old "children" who don't come around.

## Today
• • •

You forgot. You will make your choices
This morning. Even if just for yourself. You will.

Routine. There's always Routine. And it's
Safe. The pills. The animals. They need you.
It will be OK for today. You don't have a
Dog? Get a dog. It will require routine.
You need routine. It will be enough for today.

Slouch and Stumble—That sounds like
A sideshow routine. Constantly you're
Reminded stand up straight—that's
Right—shoulders back, head up—breathe
Through your nose. Slouch and Stumble
Won't do. Not in this household.

You ran a Stop Sign today. No one
Was coming, you said. But quite
Honestly, you didn't see it. What's next?
Just get up and go to work. But
There is no work. You've trained them—
Those youngsters—and there is no work
Left for you. Stop running Stop Signs.
Remember that—if you can. Put it in your
Memory book and keep it on the shelf with
All the others. Someday you plan to go
Through them—make sense of all of them.

That time will come—NOT—Why bother?
They've served their purpose. No one cares
Either. You're in the Throwing Out stage
Of life—not the organized and make sense…
The big Purge—Face it. That's where you are now.

## Don't Give Up Now
• • •

Take me with you when you go. Anything
Is better than nothing to do. Self-motivated.
There was a time—a long time—don't give
Up now. Look inward—to Silence. You
Can exist there—whole and complete.
Every day—every moment—Silence. Only do
Speak up now and then—lest you forget how.
Share what you know. Always you've shared.
It creates a link, a bond, an explosion
Of activity and direction. Activity and direction
Create the world! And you have access to it
Even as you sit in Silence. Bend yourself
A little bit. Wrap yourself completely around
An idea. Write yourself a five-star review.
You deserve it. Tell yourself why—in Silence
All the things you've done—places you have been
You'll feel better. You're not a doddering old fool.
Anyone can run a stop sign. Acceptance is an
Option. Routine has become a placeholder,
You're better than this—Talk to yourself—That
Voice that has guided you—that voice of
Desire, that voice of intuition, that voice of
Choice—every momentary choice returns if
You cease self-pity. Step out of the rut that
So easily races you along to destruction.

Live that life, and it is only a matter of time
A short matter of time, until Slipping Away
Takes over on the road to oblivion or
Whatever it is we face at the last breath.
So Breathe. Take 15 Steps forward every
Day—whatever it is—something objective.
Sleep, adequate—dream or not. Don't be
Afraid. Don't worry. Your body is your
Friend. It creates all that is you. And
Your choices create your body. Eat well—
With fascination, as every product you
Put in your mouth has an effect.

## Attitude
• • •
Notice it. Enjoy it. Move with alacrity
Even slowly if that's what it takes. Walking
Sticks, canes, wheelchairs and walkers—
Surgery for the joints—and smile between
The winces. It's the attitude that keeps you
Moving. And mentally—the need for sorrow
Is self-imposed. Free yourself up to create
This next phase of your life—reinvent
Yourself with dignity, silence, energy
And reflection. As you always have
Heretofore, swarming, dealing, building
And mentoring—taking each challenge as an
Opportunity and through it all—Taking it as it comes.

## Dignity
• • •
Reflect your way out of the rut to
Oblivion. Read your way. Play your instrument

That is you. Pluck every string. Breathe
Every tone of this new piece you are writing
Of your life. You're still here. You're still with us.
Dignity. Alacrity. And get help when you need it.
Cut yourself some slack. Give generously. Of course
We tend to become self-centered as the aches
And deficiencies call out to us demanding
Attention. An infant has only itself to
Satisfy. We have grown to satisfy the
World—in a way, our work—all around
Us. By giving we grow. It does
Not stop—this need to love, to be loved
Go all the way. Absorb the aches in
Silence: smile and gently give yourself
Away. In giving we get. In getting we
Create and gain the impulse, the energy
To give even more. Growth ensues—even
At our age. Satisfaction and the realization
That we can continue to, in our way, build
A better more joyful world for other
People. Other people draw us out. Joy
And satisfaction draw us in to well-being
And balance. Get to give. Give to get.
Inward deeply. Stay awake.
Be gentle with yourself.
Sleep takes over though. Nestle back
In bed if you have to—until routine
Takes over—which it will. It will be there.

## Resentment

• • •

Revert to the List—It's all true.
Live it. What is this resentment that

Creeps in? You did every single thing on the
List. Face it; don't ignore it. Swallow.

Swallow. Spit. Cough, and move on.
Take that tour around the yard, the room,
The woods, the block—whatever your
Boundaries allow. What are boundaries?
Useful. Keeping us in place to be able to
Focus on the matters at hand within
A manageable space. Resentment is the
Bonfire that clears out good and bad
Leaving a charred and useless structure.

## Renovation
• • •

Renovation is required. Forget it. You
Can forget it and live on in that black
And awkward smelly space. It's
Your choice. There's a peek of
Sunlight wending its way among the
Charred timbers and branches that
Were once you. Forget it. But it
Plucks its way toward you. Persistent.
Turn your head and it touches your cheek.
Like a kiss. Tell me your name. Tell me
About yourself. You can hear well, not
Altogether great, but well enough
To understand. You dribble forward opening
Your mouth to speak. The heat and
Smoke from the charred embers compete
With the sunlight—you're confused. It's
No longer clear—who did you hate? Who
Threatened you—You can't ignore that.

## Sheer Will
• • •

The sunlight on your cheeks turns into
A blaze—a full on frontal attack—
That sucks the mucous from your
Throat, your nose, your brain—
It hurts to be so blessed when
You're squirming in the negative
Ions snapping all around, crackling
In the memory of the fire you
Just this past instant walked through—
Put out with sheer will—that fascinated
You like the kiss of the sunlight
Before the full embrace—sheer light
Ripping you from the embrace of
Resentment—that caused this debacle
In the first place. Accept the kiss.
Accept the full-on frontal attack of
Light. Maybe it's God. The full energy
Of the Universe peering down at
You, entering every pore with a
Chuckle. By damn—you youngster,
In spite of yourself. In spite of yourself
You're going to be all right. It's
Such a pleasure to be here conversing
With the Sovereign who has deigned to
Come into this burned-out hell hole
You created—inadvertently through
Lack of attention. Not caring. Giving up.
Stand up and face him. He is you.
You realize. Take charge now with delight.
Get out of bed and Go! Move! Smile.
Sheer will.

## Stay Engaged
• • •
It's a new day, as the kids romped
Through the holidays—youthful energy
Takes charge focusing the oldsters
On the joy and exuberance of the
Youngsters. Joy to the world is a reality
On all levels. 9 to 91 in the same
Room—some smiling—some sleeping—
Dozing it's called, as the eyes gently
Close next to you on the sofa. Someday
That will be you, with your eyes
Closing in a lingering smile as the
Kids continue to romp—romp through
Life's demands, as you once did. It's
All right. Such a joy. Joy all around.
Beating up on yourself is not possible
In this light—in the presence of this
Contagion that is youth—delightful
Youth. Take charge now. Let yourself
Speak and participate in this discussion
About hearing aids? —Some do; some
Don't. Leave me alone—the 91-year-old
On the sofa next to you whispers.
They won't leave me alone about it.
And maybe silence is better, more
Pleasurable at 91, since it's so
Impractical around the youngsters
When they are about. Roundabout.
It's a lovely world!!! Stay engaged…

## The Metaphor
• • •

Get out of the house. Sailing—sailing—
It's time for the rejuvenation of the
Sun on the sails, the roar of the
Wind as the waves nearly overtake you
Slicing through the swells of resistance.
Responsibility raises its welcome head.
You must do this. You are in charge.
Capable and in charge, as you have been
All your adult life. The consequences
Can be dire, if the least lack of
Attention tears you away. The winches
To tighten, the tiller to resist, the balance
Required, and don't forget—don't forget
To remember. Remember is better than
Forgetting. Remember the squall just over
The horizon. It was predicted. It will
Be manageable—Shorten sail—quickly.
Prepare for the dynamite about to drop
On you out of the sky as the wind tears
At the vessel that is you—nearly
Rips the tiller from your hands
Blows you all around you, as you
Hold the course and they are safe.
The dynamite turns into sunlight after
The squall. All your crew are safe. You
Are safe and in control. Not in the
Water, but out of the water, sailing in
The metaphor that is you—you and your boat.

## Walk, Hug, Sleep
• • •

Strangulation is not an option—Too
Many horror movies—or at least the
Unwanted previews. So much better to
Wake up to the sun in the sky. Mummified
Is not an option you understand—A pharaoh
You are not—only a simple individual
Of the modern world—the civilized
Protected—as you know it—world. A walk
In the woods is one of the most grounding
Choices you can make. A hug before
You go. A hug along the way. And a
Hug when you return, before you
Pass out from the exhilaration. He was
91, you were younger. May you function
As well as he. Make the choices—or even
Better. Blow that Covid breath-o-meter. It's
An exercise you never dreamed of. Take
Each of your toes one by one. Rub and
Enjoy them—one by one. Quit while you're
Ahead. But…but…but…you could still
Have a career ahead of you…Some do. What
Should it be? Sleeping sounds pretty good.
Sleeping is not a career. It is only a choice.

Stay rested, yes. But there is—could be—
Something you really enjoy. Reading sounds
Pretty good. Read is not a career. It is only
The window into possibilities—or a complete
Diversion into mystery and imagination—
Someone else's. But it captures parts of you—
Enlivens them. Do you really want a career?

Travel could be—is—enough—to bring you
And the other—the significant one—great joy
As you romp together with your walkers
(Or maybe walking sticks)—and canes. The
Apron on that chef looks rather snug.
He eats well. His own cooking? Sitting on
The promenade deck, you get to take in
The whole scene. The expansive scene
Of the world before you. Anything to
Postpone total departure—slipping…
You don't want to. Walk. Hug. Sleep.

## Exist
• • •

Return and plan the next trip. Planning
Can be a career. Lists. Places. Things to do
You never dreamed of until you read
That book and realized that could be you.
Over and over that could, or not—be you.
Wake up a little more and it will make
More sense. That dream whatever it was
Could help you on your way—if you
Want a way. Choose. No choice is a choice.
Silence. Quiet are choices. No judgement just
Do it for a while. Exist. You will find that
It's pleasant in here. No hearing aids. Few
Friends and more. The children you paid to
Love you. That's ridiculous. We love each other
As a matter of default. It rumbles around
Inside of us. Slow down and savor every minute.

## Growing Older
• • •

A sneeze! Not a dainty hanky to the nose
Sneeze, but a full chested explosion that
Shoots a feather across the room—
Turns heads two blocks away type sneeze—
More common after Covid more than a
Year ago. Nothing one would associate
With growing older—who knows? Does
Your body still function? What do you
Notice—legs work—slightly slower. Memory
You can't deny it is slipping. You learn
To ask others about themselves to avoid
Being an old- age bore. Nether parts—forget
It. You bind them up as necessary. At
Least you can still do that for yourself.

## Alone
• • •

They trust you enough—your capabilities—
To leave you alone for a while. You
Still have a bank account. Alone becomes
A new experience—Welcome—to be with
Your thoughts. Tear out the hearing aids.
Pull on your own clothes. But then
There are the responsibilities. Cook for yourself
But don't leave the stove on—the pots will
Melt. Feed the birds—that's always a joy.
A dog is a great companion. A cat becomes
A consolation—its soft fur against your
Face. A sneeze like the one you had scares
Them all away. It sets your body
Tingling to the core—an unusual

Sensation. Not as soul-searing as the
Ones you remember that kept you alive
And balanced with another. You find your
Own way now—alone. Non-judgmental
Or you'll go nuts. The extra tingle in
Your arms is there—left over from the
Heart attack long ago. Will it return?
Maybe. All sorts of things are there to
Go wrong—to eventually fail. Better to
Fail alone--that way to avoid the solitary
Hovering of family, or friends. Maybe at
The last minute you'll welcome them,
And they do cook for you, caress you now
And then, draw you out in memories
Of the past, but they don't need you—burden
That you are. Or are you? Remember
Your friends—the old ones—older, much
Older than you, whom you helped as
They transitioned and eventually slipped
Away. Joy at caring for them. Driving them.
Bringing meals. Helping them accomplish
Listening to their dreams and memories—
That is you now—don't be a grouch—or
You really will be left alone. Right now—
This is merely a hiatus as the others go
Away—take their trips without you. Feed the
Dogs. Enjoy your routine. Stop the
Sniveling—it's definitely unbecoming!

## Money
• • •

The youngsters have done it. More money
Than you can imagine drops in your lap.

The business deals you trained them in so
Long ago—they know what they are doing.
How do you feel? Money's ephemeral.
You're grateful. The vision paid off.
The patience paid off. Going for what you
Wanted paid off. It always does—
Or so it feels at the moment. The youngsters—
You were 55 once—flying through your
Power period. You never gave up. You
Grinned and faced every committee, every
Official, every opponent that you
Invariably turned into a friend—or at
Least a neutralized force. Life's Force
Was a given—It's still a given—Measured
In money. Sometimes…. Money is ephemeral.

## Envisioning
• • •

You are cared for—You cared for—such
Is the way things go—Give to get. Get to
Give. Stay out of the moldy corners. Go
For the light of full exposure—ALWAYS.
It doesn't mean you don't keep a
Confidence. It doesn't mean you splatter
Your vision against the pavement to be
Trampled. You coddle it, encourage
It and watch it grow into being—this
Business, this job, this drive—whatever
It is—or was, in which you excelled—
And then envisioned it gradually, as they
Grew—in your youngster—friend or
Child—those whose lives you touched
And whose life and lives touched yours.

## Ephemeral Energy
• • •
And they've done it. Made the deal. Planned
The approach. Built the network. Worried
The structure of their life into being, and
It affects you now. You're old. You've
Given it all—or so much of it away, and
The youngsters, the children, those you
Know are a success, and you gave; now
You get, you benefit. Give it away
Again—money, it's ephemeral energy that grows
In place as you give it again to other
Lives—other visions. Whatever the amount
Small or large it will have an effect on
The future, the friends you have made, the
Ones unborn, this generation and the next
And the next. It was done for you—the mentors,
Father, mother, friend, bankers—guides who
Attracted you—created the you of you—
The joy of watching you grow, and it's your
Turn. Fifty units, fifty thousand, fifty
Million. It's your turn now. Give it away—
Ephemeral energy to the Universe. Watch
And feel satisfaction as the Life Force
Moves through you, dribbles through you,
Explodes through you to the world.

## Nourishment
• • •
And then you'll forget. But those around you
Will remember and benefit, and then they'll
Forget. Nourishment for a while—the short
While we're here. Here in this moment

Of a year, fifty years, a hundred years,
We'll build our pyramids and then
The sand will come—blowing—covering
Protecting our memory, to be uncovered
Decades, centuries ahead. Scholars will see,
But who cares? It's in the now, the now
Of the moment that it matters—nudging
Nourishment onto friends, family, organizations
That make a difference because they are
Alive, active, working and surviving. You
Survived. Who helped you? Those who
Built the roads—the network in which
You struggled at first and then thrived
For the moments you had traversing the
Paths and byways tying it all together.

And you learned it. Others showed you.
You turned inward and in patience
Developed the visions, the tools the
Friends, the vehicles, the lover and
Affection that surrounded you, accompanied
You in our exploration of the roads,
Paths, and byways that make society.
It was a great fit. You—them—they
You—love, affection, and success.

## Give, Get, Grow, Gone
• • •

It all mattered. Enjoy the memory. That's
Easier and more fun, and more likely
Than remembering to put the top on the
Water bottle before you knock it over.
The vision that was you is easier

Than remembering the name of who
You're talking to—this one in front of
You. That's just the way it is. But
Giving all you have is a great feeling—
Money—and then it's gone, out there
Growing somewhere—benefiting the
Roads, the buildings, the byways of
This network that is society. And you
Helped cause it—Cause it—or just
Participated, because the whole
Process gave you pleasure—great
Pleasure this life of yours—nourished
By others, explored and created by
Yourself learning to manipulate this
Life Force through your inner workings,
As it was meant to be. Silence, duty, direction
Cemented in this past of love, oozed out
Of you and helped make this society, the
Neighborhood with its friends, neighbors and
Barking dogs. Muzzle the beasts. But they too
Are your best friends—and we all bark
Now and then. Grow, grow—
And then you're gone. Give get. Grow Gone.

## Gone
. . .

This gets complicated. Your friend is gone
The one with the back-scratcher. Can you
Remember his final days before they
Slipped Away? Friends came. Assets
Slipped away to family. No bills. Much
To talk about—all the good done, people
Helped. Who got the ashes—it doesn't

Matter. Gone. Another friend—no
Assets. Caring for through—say it… Cancer.
Deep caring. Financial caring—Years of caring.
No family. A loving liability in your home.
All the bills—you supported. All that you knew
Of. They at last did slip away—gone home
To another country and there they had no—
No bills—but you did. One day they
Came—a year's worth—hospital, doctor.
You're not responsible, but they came
To your address. All at once. And you
Opened them. This person that was, was
Your ward so to speak. Thousands. Who
Pays? Deceased. Easy to say. Easy to
Write. They were old. They slipped away
Simply not communicating what was
Going on. Were they, were they not your
Ward so to speak—a 70-year-old plus
Dependent. Why didn't they tell you?
Mail is a private matter until you die.
What right did you have to open it—
But you did. Deal with the hospital.
How do they handle bills of the deceased?
If it were a good friend who was owed,
Would you settle up? Probably. The Hospital
Has kept you going for years—two decades.
Check with them. There's the legal, the ethical,
And there is friendship and memory. Push this
Forward to resolution. Fat is no excuse.
Lethargy is no excuse. Vitality is in the
Balance—or so it seems. Tidy—that is
How you would like to leave your affairs.
Tidy with good memories. You have closed

The books and the attics, the basements,
The garages of parents on both sides.
It's not embarrassing. We all leave at
Some point. Decisions will have to be made.

## Stuff
. . .

Who gets what? Stuff—more stuff—the
Joys of the middle-class. Do we need it
Everyone needs it. We eat it. We sleep with it.
We fondle it, play with it, share it, identify
With it, drive it, wreck it, fix it, give it away,
Hoard it, see it, write it, sell it, thrive in
The midst of it. We love our stuff. It's who
We are—unless we've found a deeper meaning.
Silence is compatible with stuff. Action
And direction secure more stuff. Silence
Helps us as a resource to put it to its best use
For ourselves and for others. Settle up. Pay the bill.
Money is stuff too.

## Fatigue
. . .

Go along your way. Thirsty—water courses
Through you bringing energy, not quite pushing
Out the fatigue. Why fatigue? It's more
Lately. Pushing back against activity. Routine
Steps back in to help. Thank God for bodily
Functions. Thank God for smiles. And animals
That make noises. When you're alone you're
Not alone. And the people will be back. They've
Always come back, until they don't.
Then you go see them. Silence and alone

Is all right. It's not the end of the world—
Your world begins there—return us there.

## Anxious
• • •
Nothing to be anxious about. Anxious.
Hungry pets are anxious. Anxious because
They are hungry. They want affection,
Attention. They may need to go out. Being
Anxious is one way to express your need
For something you don't have. Once you
Get what you want, you're no longer anxious—
At least until the next want comes along.

## The Lists
• • •
Work at it. We want. We always want.
We have the luxury of being literate—able
To write down what we want. We may
Need someone to open the door to let us out
Or we may still be able to do that little
Chore for ourself. If we write it down—
What we want—and focus on it—we
Will likely get it. At least we'll remember it.
Hence the lists. Hence the silence—bodily
Functions aside—they're important of
Course and must be satisfied—unbound
And satisfied, but in Silence we can
Extend into the future. This, this, this,
And this. They're on the list now. We
Know we want them. No one can take
Away our memory then. And memory
Leads to action, thoughts lead to action.

Action leads to success, and we can
Still walk over the log on the path, or onto
The worksite, into the shop, into the
Office, onto the assembly line where the
Youngsters have taken over. We're not
Needed, but we wanted to go there and
That feels like success for a little while
Until the next need nudges forward.

We read the list, and yes. We remember
Again. We want this. Now go get it.
It's OK to arrange to have it brought to us—
Where we are. Then we don't have to move
About as much. We can sit right here
And ramble in comfort. Let them bring
It to us on a tray. That's success. Take
The trip and forget about everything.
Get up and drive away—oh—where
Are the keys? Lost forever—so sit back and relax.
At least they haven't taken them away—
Or have they? It's hard to remember.

## Faithful Old Friend
• • •

Dog tired. My dog is 108 in dog years. Hard
To believe—faithful old friend. He
Stumbles. He can no longer hear. Help him
Stand. Lift his hind quarters. He walks.
In the woods he still perks up for the treats
And can quicken his pace very slightly
To come for a bite. The others lick his face
And help heal the sores. Everybody loves
Him. Clean up after him as necessary.

Reilly, Molly, Zeke, Zinka, Bailey,
Bryn—so many have gone before—
Misty, Baxter, Nick, Bootsie—an endless
List of friends you have held in your
Heart and in your arms as the Vet
Fondles them with you and gives them
Their last shot. They sit on the shelf for
Years and eventually get committed to
The back yard. Enough joy has been
Engendered in those 108 years to make
It all worthwhile. And your life? May
You live as long—engendering joy—
Some days yes—some days—not likely.
But that's OK. It is what it is. You
Take It As It Comes—Smile. Silence.

## Concentration
• • •

And the grimaces that come up? Like
A little kid—biting his tongue to focus
On completely the task at hand—you
Realize you scowl when you're
Filling the dog dish—not from anger. Not
From frustration—but just to get it
Right. Or cleaning the bird cages or
Washing the dishes—you catch yourself
Like a little kid making faces. It makes
You laugh when you realize it, so
You talk to yourself—remind yourself
That you know this task. Equanimity
And a smooth brow used to be the
Norm. Relax and do the task—no need
For this grimace of concentration—

It's routine for crying out loud. But
Still you have to catch yourself
Until someone comes in the room and
You realize you have to lighten up. Its
All right. No need to be so hard on yourself.

## Talk to Yourself
• • •

Settle into routine. And when that is
Disturbed…take a deep breath and face
The New. 108 dog years. You might
Make it. You've learned to write the
Check—reread it—set it aside for a
While, come back to it, compare it to the
Bill, correct the errors you made—you
Misspelled the name, reversed the
Numbers, the date is last year, not this—
You rewrite, review. It's just routine
Now—the new routine. And it does help
If you frown while you're writing—even
Grimace—a little. Talk to yourself. It will help.

## A New Year
• • •

Turn the page. Turn over a new year.
It's all there. Somewhere inside you.
Draw on it. To give back. It's your turn
For a while. Self-centered. That's just the
Way it is. Forthright. Forgetful. But you…
Drooling is a necessary phenomenon.
Dogs drool. Cats rule. Something like
That. Move out of the house at least
Once a day—fresh air, health, biting cold
In the snow.

## Red Snowsuit
• • •

You remember in your Red snowsuit
Crawling on your mother's
Back, as she lay on the sled. You were three,
Maybe four, at the top of the thrilling
Hill with the curves and white and
Big hemlock hedges aside the steep hill.
No cars, just the thrill of your short
Life, and she shot off on the Flexible
Flyer with the red runners, steering
Madly as the snow sprayed over and
Around you—seared in your memory,
Racing, flying full speed for some long
Minutes—a long hill how do you stop?
Fearful, but Mother is there steering like
A Banshee whatever that was at three or
Four—down curves, along hedges—spray--
White delight fear and fun, at the
Last curve a slight turn and—shooting
Up the neighbor's driveway to a safe stop at
The top of his hill. Never, ever to forget those
Moments.

## Decades Ago
• • •

She was fearless while Daddy
Was off to war. Decades ago. Standing
And rocking in your white metal crib
Tearing pieces of wallpaper dried in small
Sheets off the wall—how satisfying it was—
Your career lay ahead of you—demolition
Of whatever you could get your hands on—
Buildings, people, marriages, nasty boys

Who tried to cut in front of you in
Line. You learned to frown and scowl
And be hurt until she held you in her
Arms—your mother. Stay with her until
She died out from under you far away.
Soul searing—but expected—no, never
Expected. The inner you never expects to
Lose her. Never to turn her loose. But Daddy
Came home and took over. So strange to
Think back. And he's gone too, And you—
You're still here. Still here—only partially
Gone—down that hill with the snow
Flying around you until you come to
A full stop in the neighbor's driveway. And
Indeed—it was so scary along the way
But you held on—delighted in some strange
Way to be scared, but secure and all
Your life you've been scared but secure
And seeking the next adventure. That's just
The way it is with you—and it's coming!!

## A Blank

• • •

It's frightening to walk into a room—around
You are people you know, but don't know.
You've done it all your life—fearlessly facing
Unknown situations, managing until they
Swayed and evolved and you come out,
Came through—if not on top—at least
One of the group—swaying with the group,
Directing, taking charge as your parents
Used to do. Getting things done. Always
Moving forward—getting things done. And

Then you walk into a room and everyone
Knows who you are. You may not know
Them. But they know you. Know of you.
It's satisfying of course—a boost to who
You are—think you are—know for certain
Who you are, and you don't give it a
Thought anymore. And today you walk into
The room—the room—the space, the encounter
And there they are—these people around you
You've come to know, come to respect, come
To love and care for. All the links are
Made—they are there—except it's a Blank
And you're uncertain—form and function
Take over. The sociable hellos, smiles, hugs
The yes of courses. It's all there. They're
All there. Except you're not. Not at least
In the way you were—confident and inside
Knowing with absolute certainty this is the way
Things should be. Who are these people? You
Can name some of them. –Oh, they do this.
They do that. This one's here to take care of you.
This one doesn't smell particularly good—
Or is that you? Oh, s…! But don't use
That word. Smile. Accept. It's different
Now. But you're still able and friendly
And glad to be here. Noticed again—sort of.

## A Dream
• • •

You walk down the lane past the old
Cars with grass growing up around them…
It's a dream. But you love it. Past an
Old house in the woods. They're serving

Food. Healthy, nourishing food, but it will
Take a while to prepare. And they know
You. Act like you know them—friendly
And take up from where you left off.
But it's a dream—in a dream you wake up.
And you feel good. Secure. Refreshed
And ready to move on. Move back to the
Place you know. And you wake up again
And you don't know—not for sure, not
For certain. You're in control. Find your
List. You can write down their names. They
Know yours. Get to know them. In a different
Soundless way. You don't hear that well
Anyway—What? What! They told you
That before. A million times—put in your
Hearing aids. Between the lists and the
Hearing aids you'll be OK.

## Just Be
. . .

This may be enough. Slipping Away.
Change direction. Stop all together.
Live in the moment with the things, the
Places—forget the places—just be. The people
You know. You do know them. No need
To forecast your demise any longer. When
You focus on something—that's what you
Get. Just be. You've made your
Statement. The children are launched.
Your friends are still there and around.
You've pointed out the idiosyncrasies
Of old age—at least your own old age.
Wrap it up. Throw it away. Don't go

Back. You don't go forward by going back.
Creativity will open up to you again. Projects—
You've done your projects—a lifetime of projects.
But what are you if you don't have
Projects, plans, goals—always living for
What you want. What are you?... Stop now.

## Dharma
• • •

Find out. Deep inside. You've been trained
To go there too. It's a major part of your
Life. You've used the meditation to make
Yourself successful. It has been the
Basis of strong, successful, ethical,
Action—based on your desire to create
A better more joyful world for others—
Your dharma as you see it—as
You've lived it. People around you will
Find their own Old Age. Let it go now, for
Yourself. Live Afresh. Afresh with joy
In your heart—for the moment—the moments
As they open up for you. Relax the planning.
See what it's like to really just be here
Now. Not the now as a steppingstone to
Desire and action. Stop all that. This
Is new. For you it is new. See where
It goes…How it feels—SLIPPING AWAY
Into the moment. This new reality that
Surrounds you now and is sufficient.

You've lived through OLD AGE—now
Take LIFE AFRESH…

## Part Three

⊙ ⊙ ⊙

# LIFE AFRESH

## Frustration

• • •

It's an attitude. The shampoo's gone.
The conditioner's only half gone
Frustration? —No—So buy a smaller bottle
Of the shampoo to match what's left
Of the conditioner. No frustration—a
Very minor feeling of elation. It's a
Beginning. The pills so neatly distributed
In their green box—enough for a week
Are down to their last compartment.
Frustration? —No—sort from the pill
Bottles and replenish your weekly
Assortment. If necessary, order more
Bottles. You know they help you.
Face the reality—the routine of
Getting up every day. Washing, dressing—
Pills, a little exercise. You sense
The alternative, and it's not pleasant.

## Choosing

• • •

There's a positive path and a negative
Path, and you can choose—smiles—
Engagement. Caring for someone else.
Caring for yourself. Or you can choose
Wandering in the wilderness of
Loneliness. You've done it all your
Life—Engaging. Making things happen.
Thrifty, but generous. Knowing where
You are—what to do—Buy that small
Bottle of shampoo.

## Advancing the Cause
• • •

"Advancing the cause"—that's what the
Younger one so close and dear to your heart
Calls it. The cause—of wisdom, happiness,
Health, and wealth—of all the things you
Want and have wanted. Advancing the cause.
It's the getting up versus rolling over. It's the
Walk with the critters. It's the gentle meals
That satisfy but don't overdo. And yes, it's
The hug in the morning, the pat during the day,
And the embrace at night before you go
The separate ways of old age. To sleep.
It's the good morning and caring for another—
Even older. It's the furry cats, the raucous
Parrots, and the diminishing dogs, as they
Peel off and leave after their 12 and 13,
And maybe 14 years. Sad days—but happy
In the remembering and the pictures. It's
Too—the planning, the lists, the details of the
Trips—where, when, who. Around the world!

Yes—you've saved. Or next door just to be
Friendly—the getting out of you—your
Shell, your dwelling, small or large. It's the
Music and the Theatre, the events that have
Couped up for so long due to this Covid—
Two years "lost"—Lost to memory—
Or so it feels. It is great fullness expressed
To the younger one so close to your heart,
To the children—gratefulness for the attention
They do give so drawn up in their own
Families, and loves, and dreams, and

Successes—the boys, ages 9 and 14 just skied
"Black Diamond"—bombing the slopes
Without hesitation. No, the grandson
Will not be continuing with college. He
Loves working. The granddaughter is
Heading to Charlotte after graduation.
And your friends—Yes, they will accompany
You on a trip this summer. And your
Own mental state—the mold is gone
The clean-up is remaining—is it half
Full or half empty. Choose the full.

The cup is not seeping away half empty,
It is filling and half full—of the dreams
And all the choices to be made for
Growth, joy, and contentment—
Advancing the cause—for yourself and
Others—those around you and those
Under attack from enemies, from
Old age, from despair. Nourish the
Cosmos with all your heart—filling the
Cup daily as you turn in to Silence
To the deepest realization of Transcendence.
Despair is too easy. Keep your corner clean.
Open your heart fully. Every moment.
Advance the Cause!

## Security
• • •

Life Afresh—Accept your greatest challenge.
It's always been that way since childhood.
A legacy of your parents, who carved their
Way through World War II—fighting, the Philippines,

Japan—a hero who never talked about it.
The security, surrounded by the love that
Engulfed you even though you didn't know
What it was, as you grew like a plant.
It was water, encouragement, guidance
And propping up when need be. Old Age
Didn't take over—well it did for a while—
Covid, mold, old age—the Debilitators!

## Reassertion of Vitality
• • •

A creative trip—you'd decided even
Before you both left for another part of
The world—to abandon old age—for this
Reassertion of vitality—this relaxed and
Stilled appreciation of the moment—you called it
"Life Afresh" and you realized one day
Later that you had purloined this phrase
From a box of laundry detergent, which
Doesn't make it any less valid—only cleaner—
Like laundry you both had to do at the
Laundromat weekly, since the basement
Along with your washer/dryers was off
Limits due to the sluggish mold remediation.

## Greatest Challenges
• • •

A curative trip that proved to be the
Ultimate cure for debilitation,
Self-pity, and the fatigue and self-imposed
Attitude of loneliness in the "Old Age" phase
Of your life. And now you realize
Attitude is everything. It's fighting back

With gentleness, fun and joy, that opens
Up when you realize that, yes, you have
This limitation, that limitation (and that
You've always had limitations,) but you
Have transcended them by turning to
Silence—to the acceptance of Life's Force
Flowing through, summoned by desire.
Reflection and determination of what
You want, and you have guided yourself
To what you want by recognizing and
Accepting your "Greatest Challenges,"
Whatever you recognize them to be.
That became the key that opened the
Pathway to using your skills, your
Experience at whatever level you were
To move forward, to grow, to achieve,
And as you developed—to experience
That we truly gain our happiness by
Living, giving our life and energies to
And toward a better, more joyful
World for other people. Society. We are
A member. Even in our shored up
Old Age, we are a member. The principles
Still work—Face it. You've got to do this!
Make the list. *What do you want?* Accept your
Greatest Challenges. It's Life's Force— "Afresh!"

## Capability
• • •

Capability—Projects and possibilities open
Up as you realize you do have it. It
It has not disappeared with sagging memory.
Remember trying to do the math in your

Head. There's always been a limit—a
Recognition of the complexity involved
In this one, and you picked up the paper
And pen to keep order and arrive at
The solution. And the limits have changed.
So you pick up the paper and pen perhaps
Sooner. The calculator, the blessed
Computer, all shore your confidence and
Enable you to function and solve
With capability and confidence. The lists
Are OK. The tools that keep you steady.
The walking stick that keeps you steady.
You don't always need it, but when the
Terrain is rough, challenging, you take
It along. Accepting that greatest challenge
Can be getting to the next rise ahead on
The track. The daily walk, the exercise—
Clear your head and restore your body
And your confidence, that indeed it does
Function and is capable and you haven't
Given up. Take your friend and neighbor
And drive them to see their 90-year-old
Dad—a day away. Invite your friends
A few at a time to show the pictures
As you project them from your latest
Curative trip. Wear your hearing aids.
It's OK and will ease it for everyone.

## Acceptance
• • •

Wrinkled skin and a few sags won't
Hinder helping one of the several social
Groups solve their problems—construction,

Financing, building—that you're involved in.
Rewrite, pick it apart when it still
Doesn't make sense or add up correctly
On the third try. You accept—things take
Longer, go slower, but the answer is
In there and you know eventually you
Will find it. Age commands a certain
Respect and always has—the older
Kids on the playground, the mentor who
Has been there before, and it is you, if
You have found a way to navigate
Through the limitations we face or will
Face, as we tune-up and adapt to the
Barking dogs, the financial dilemma,
That stop sign you missed—all with
Acceptance that opens up continuing—
Versus frustration and more frustration,
Until you close down in frustration, and
That's the beginning on the end of the road.
Acceptance, adaptation, in reorganizing—
Until you've got it right and can
Move through the challenges with
Capability and confidence.

## A Refreshing Step
• • •

Out and about. It's been two years since
You took your dearest one and a few others
To a movie in a theatre. Movies at home
Have been refreshing and supportive, but to
Sit in the theatre—500 plus seats was a
Thrill—holding the hand of the one dearest to
You—the lights dim—the trailers, ads,

And now the film. 500 seats. You sit in the
Center—the perfect spot in this complex of a
Dozen theatres. There was no one at the box
Office—you bought tickets at the concession
Stand. No one took your ticket. You walked up
The ramp and found Theatre 5. Chose your seats.
Waited…. And no one else was there. So few people…
Would they run the movie—of course they would.
It's probably all computerized anyway.
But no one else was about. No one else. No bustle.
No popcorn—although we did have the choice.
Covid. The whole society is recovering. We
Enjoyed it. We'd go again. Gradually life
Will return to normal. For all of us—those of
Us who are still here. Out and about. It was
A refreshing step—a willed step into *Life Afresh*.

## Activity
• • •

This is new territory. You'd thought to let go of
The planning—live in the moment—the
"Be here now."—But you've always "Been
Here Now." And you've done it in balance with
Pleasing, considered, planned, and often spontaneous
Activity—Yes, be here now. But it doesn't
Mean dropping out. The life of the recluse
Suits some who have chosen it as a
Spiritual path. There's a monastery
Several houses down the road along the lake.
A few monks out feeding the ducks,
Serving the church in the nearby Village.

You have been taught in the

Vedic tradition—the life of a householder--
The life of action, is as valid a way to
"Enlightenment," as the life of a recluse.
That was new to you fifty years ago.
It was eye-opening, and it supported
And settled you, and forever since
You have turned inward into silence
And transcending and sprung forth into
Lists and desires, projects you felt should
Be done—and did—never wavering
From finding and expanding into your
Greatest challenges—and it has worked. It has
Opened up the world to you, until Covid,
Old age, and mold slapped you down.

## In Balance
• • •

And the younger one so close and dear
To your heart has supported and guided
You back to normalcy. No more slouching
And stumbling. No more wavering and withdrawing.
Stand straight. Use your walking sticks when
You need them. Rest—even nap occasionally—but
Continue "Advancing the Cause"—accepting your
Challenges. Move forward in balance—Out and about.
One little brain, one little body linked
To the Cosmos. That's the way it is—and
It can make a difference in the world.
See all the individuals who have changed
The world—built the Pyramids, preached
The sermons—yes, started wars. Is that part
Of the Cosmos? Unfortunately, yes. Good and bad
Make up our lives—make up our societies. We

Can't be blind to it—only do our own part—
Follow our own *dharma*—that beautiful
Word signifying our duty in the world.

## Linked to the Cosmos
• • •

Desire is the key to unlocking our *dharma*.
What do we want? Recognize it. State it.
Even in our Old Age—even probably on our
Death bed we can state it, desire it, accept it—
With peace and joy in our hearts—continuing
On as we always have since we first
Ate our pablum, crawled and walked,
Grew and became. Became…Becoming…

It never ends. In the world it never ends.
Our little planet, interdependent in the
Cosmos, our little ball in the sky of the
Universe. So small and fragile, and we are
Part of it—the consciousness that keeps it all
Spinning, orbiting—we are part of it.
Interdependent even in good and bad
Wrath and love, support and devastation of
Ourselves and others—all part of it—never ending.
So take heart. Enjoy the moment. Use it
To plan and act for the future if you're so
So inclined. Use it to expand and interact
For yourself and whatever you find in
That inner space that is you, if you are so inclined.
Eventually we'll blast out of that space
That is us—in success and glory, or in
Deepest silence and acknowledgement that
We are whoever we are, and it is all good.

Or evil takes us down and maybe there is a
Hell. For some people you wish there is a
Hell and they were in it now. Causing so
Much hurt as they are with their bombs
And their greed. Sorry, but *Damn* them to Hell.

The rest of us struggle, and aid, and send thoughts
Of help but not bombs in return.
One little brain, one little body. That's
All we are. Some of us bring bombs,
Some of us bring peace and joy to others.
It's difficult. It's maddening. It's
Death and destruction for some. There has
Always been a sword, a knife, a big rock
Creating havoc humankind to humankind. Will
There ever not be? Struggle yourself.
Society at its best will keep you safe.
At its worst—misshapen. One little body,
One little brain linked to the Cosmos. It can
Make a difference in the world—
For good or evil. You choose.

## Latent Power
• • •

Is there power in the winter woods with
The snow breathing lightly, quivering so quietly
On every branch—a fabric mystical in its
Peace and tranquility—the dark big dogs, the
Color of tree bark darting, loping across the
White on the ground, tree to tree—but is there
Power there? Imagine it felled and sawn.
Cleared as it is in the fields that begin
Just at the woods edge. There's certainly latent

Power in the earth—waiting to grow crops
The trees by some are considered "a crop"—
Even in the randomness and disarray of the
Forest—latent power to burn for heat, latent
In their power to be sawn and trimmed for lumber
That builds where we live—where we work,
And play—those structures. There's immediate
Power in the beauty, peace—tranquility the
Woods bring to us. Rejuvenating body and
Spirit. No denying its power, quiet as it
Surrounds us on the path snow covered.

We won't saw it and burn it, but we will
Tuck it away to draw from later in its
Raw beauty as a memory—a nourishing
Memory that gives us power because there is
Such beauty in the world. It's a roundabout
Path that engulfs us—but there is beauty,
There is power there; there is the path.
There is order in the disorder of the branches
With their snow and the randomness.
The dark, furry images—"brown trees"
On legs loping, sniffing, running about.
We draw from it all.

## Power Abounds
• • •

Another day we drive to Niagara Falls—
To take a friend half a day's drive because
She has never seen it. Niagara—
When our Swedish friends come
They want to see Nee-ah-ga'-rah
Falls. So we take them. And there is no

Denying—Power abounds—Power surrounds
Us—roars at us, deafens us and
Threatens to sweep us away. That is the
Thrill! Oh there's beauty, plenty of raw
Beauty, but it pales beside the power
Of the rushing water as wide as a country,
As massive as the Great Lakes all
Roaring at once to get through—
Crowding to leap over the precipice, the
Escarpment to the river below.
Older than the human race most likely.

It's not the woods. But it sears the memory
In a different way—peace, tranquility—
If you could silence it, that's there. But
It ROARS, unforgettably. The woods don't
Roar, they sear you with silence. The
*FALLS ROARS!!* And stimulates you with
Its thrilling embrace of power sucking you
In and down in your imagination. Tuck it
Away and draw from it later—Forever.

## Self Control
• • •

Withdraw at those times you feel hurt.
Don't lash out. Don't pout like a child.
Refrain from lashing out when they
Speak too loudly—too distinctly—forming
Their words with their teeth so you will
Hear them. Self-control wins out—finally.
You got a C-in self-control in grades
4-7, but you finally won out against
Yourself—no, with yourself. It's all

Fine now. You've gotten better now. Hearing
Is not your strong suit, but you're getting
Better in this new mode of Life Afresh.

## Vitality
• • •

It's OK. You did run another STOP sign,
But with the radar you can still drive 80—
There's vitality in it. Speed is a salve
For whatever ails you. Speed and Arnica
For the bumps and bruises. Five little pills
Under your tongue—or smear on the gel at
The precise location—Try it—you recommend
To your friends for their bumps and bruises—
Arnica, the miracle salve from the Health Food
Store. Look inside. Time passes. You feel better.

Look ahead…Some of your best friends are
Twenty years—maybe just ten or twelve
Years older than you. You look at them and
You see them as inspiration. They look at
You and see you as inspiration—Life
As it is going to be. Life as it has been.
Roar forward with assurances. We
Are all still vital—traveling, thinking,
Solving problems, sharing solutions
Some with just ourselves—some with society.
Vitality is still there, and we recognize
It—reinforce and celebrate it in each
Other from our differing vantage points.

Twelve years to go. Twelve years back.
It was like this. It will be like this

Except for Uncle G—who made the
Decision last week to forgo Dialysis—
And another to forego the cancer
Treatment—and then it is just a matter of
Time—but it's always just a matter of time.
Cram in as much as you can, before you
Wave and depart for uncharted territory.
Have a good time. That's what friends are
For—Love, recognition, mutual support, and
Fun together—friends and those we love.

So don't pout. Hoist your sails, put on
The Hearing Aids and take your friends along
All those you love and care for. And they
Care for back to you, even sometimes through
Clenched teeth. It's a jolly old time together.
C-in self-control aside. You're strong now.
Arnica soothes the bumps. The woods are
Silent. The Falls roar. You overcame the sensation
Of wanting to leap into the power of the rushing
Current of the blue water and over the precipice--
You chose dry land and continued—Vitality—
Self-control.

## Too Hot
• • •

A clear channel to a full-blown Tangle.
How can one little body/brain make a
Difference when halfway across the world
The news crumples a country. What will be left?
Follow the scams—send this—send that.
Don't get involved. That's not possible.
Stop watching. What good will that do?

Swerve around and go another direction.
What good will that do? Look into the eyes
Of a three-year-old. The soup's too hot. She
Refuses, as she looks into the steam pouring off it.
Sweetie—just take a small spoonful from
Around the edges. Her father says—No,
Once too hot, it's always too hot. She
Won't eat it.

## The Tangles
• • •

It's safe here. A small world.
And it's being twisted and blown into shards
And a body count—a tangle of despair
On the other side. Routine. Lists. Patience.
Order the tangle as best you can in
Silence. Seen from space we're a small
Globe, orbiting steadily through history.
We've been there. We'll be back. It's turning.
Like a heart rate—Good will surge through
Our veins again. Patience. Breathe deeply.
What will the leaders do? There are many
Good people riding with us as we orbit
The sun. See what today brings. Quiver and
Cry. Pour out good thoughts. And follow the thread.
Tangles eventually unravel if enough attention
Is brought to bear.

## Let Us In
• • •

Hey guys—let us in…let us work.
Society in shambles. Recovering from
Covid. Recovering from the big dole.

Four people quit last week. Higher
Wages, benefits all foregone. Three
People interviewed. Two agreed to take
The jobs. Monday came. They didn't show.
They didn't call. Nothing. Business in
Distress. Society in distress. Are we in
Shock? Hey guys—let us in! We'll
Work. The borders are closed. We've
Had our mass migration. First, second,
Third generation—you're one of us now.
Didn't you go to school. Yes. Can't you
Just play your video games and
Cash your check. Yes. Some few are
Working, some few are loyal hard-working,
But overall, the parts don't come—
The big delay. We're too old for this. Why
Can't we count on you? At the lowest
Ends—don't you know how important
You are. Taking hold and growing
If you can. Never mind. No one's
Irreplaceable. Hey guys…we'll let you in
If we can find you. This big malaise
Can't last forever. We're going to build
Our buildings. Make the repairs. Take care
Of our commitments. Produce our products.
Sheer will. And hope we balance Society.

## So Much Noise
• • •

The great leap. With the first few notes
In the theatre you knew you were alive.
The balcony began shaking. Crowds moving
In unison at each jarring note—each beat.

# LIFE AFRESH

You were a kid again. Lights flashing
On the stage, on the audience—a
Packed house. You made it happen. You
Bought a ticket. Hell, you even bought
A theatre a dozen years ago to bring it
Back to life—spurred on by your social-
Minded, true love. Can an instrument—
Six of them, make so much noise?!

You wanted to come—by yourself—
OK, for the experience, and it roared at
You. Note by ferocious note. Beat by beat
By beat by beat, until everything
Shook and the smoke from the floor
Below wafted in the lights through the
Dancing crowds at the front of the stage.
Fun was not the word. Abstract—
Removed from reality—so powerful
5-10-30 minutes for the first song, piece,
Jumble—whatever it was coming at you.
Making you feel—there—shocked—determined
To ride it out. And in the silence, as the
Band stopped, you realized and drew
A parallel. The thousand people
Murmuring between the walls—the
"Collegiate-Gothic" Arches of this unique
Space—the murmuring was like the
Water rushing by in the river above
The falls. Rapids. Ne-ah-ga'rah—

Rushing. Snow. Mist. Last week. Ahead
Was the precipice. You were alive
Walking beside the murmuring rapids

And with the first note of the next
Piece—CRASH!! You were at the
Precipice. The sticks, the logs, the
Debris was tumbling on your head
As over the precipice you went.
Stone and boulders fell with you and
One with them, you descended in
The crash, the roar, the strength.
That funny smelling smoke…
You were alive—you were falling
Into a hell of your own making—
You came, you allowed yourself—
Swept along and now irretrievably
Swept over the precipice as you
Munched on your cookie from the
Refreshment stand—alone in your
Seat at the balcony's front edge—
The peak and the precipice that you
Also enjoyed between bites just
Realizing this was the Arts, Dining
And Entertainment that help keep
Your little downtown alive—a Dark Star
Roaring over the falls and you with it.
Society alive in its own way—
In spite of itself.

## Who Wants Life on a Leash
• • •

Sunday is the day for dogs—actually every
Day is. Routine. Living beings who need
You. You don't leave without caring
Or seeing that they are cared for.
In return—sitting among them—in

Your lap—stroking—licking—stretching out.
It's always been this way—another being,
To care for—be responsible for—a joy
In itself. And your neighbors all know
Them—they're at our house—
On the porch—we're feeding them biscuits—
On my way—and they jump in the back
Of the SUV—the dog SUV with blankets
And towels for the mud. Next time we'll
Walk them on the two-mile trail through
The woods to the waterfall—and you do.
They come back with you tuckered out.
But it's all an act, as they come with
You to the house—great—and then…
Veer off for a run to the lake—the
Heck with breakfast—the heck with you.
Civilized dog "parents"—keep their
Critters on a leash. But that's no fun…
Four (now three) big chocolate brown
Critters walking sedately beside you when
There are acres of woods—trees to sniff,
Streams to cross, freshly manured fields
To roll in? Who wants life on a leash!

## We're OK
• • •

Net worth is an ephemeral measure.
Every year the pressure valve blows
And spews dollar signs across the page.
The banks want to know. How many are
There? Where are they hidden—
Full disclosure—always—a cleansing
Of sorts, as you order and arrange

Meticulous from statements, deals,
Transactions—this was mine—that
Was yours, as we shook it all up doing
Our best to survive Economic Injury
Disaster and here's a loan to help out
As so many didn't pay, couldn't
Pay, as Covid ripped through our country—
No product, no orders, no rents, no
Evictions—it's all ephemeral this
Construct we live in together. We don't
Work. We can't work. We must work
Some of us, to keep our sanity, our
Own food on the table of life. Why
Won't you work? Are we naturally lazy?
Don't think so. Your nature—our
Natures are designed to survive—to gasp
For air, and the oximeter slipped over
Your finger tells you how much air
You're entitled to today—at this moment—
The post heart attack—post Covid—
Enjoy-life-moment. What is your
Net Worth—you've worked hard—despite
The threats—despite mal-functioning
Body and brain—you're out of it now,
And the Net Worth spews across the
Page—letting the banks know—society
Know—we're through it now. We're OK

## Spewed Across the Page
• • •

And you know—now—once a year
Even for the past 50 years, as value
And growth have soared, enabling you,

Your family, your little corner
Of society to benefit. If only it could
Reach across the world—the ephemeral
Vibes and make it all OK. Missiles
And bombs continue to drop, wrenching
Your heart—but here the numbers
Say everything is settled and back to
Normal. Growth appears normal.

It always has been, until a 90-year-old
Relative unearthed a ration book to
Show how much butter you could buy
In World War II—that was yesterday—
A shock—you were born, and here's
How much butter—or was it margarine then,
Your family was entitled to? Net Worth
Rains down on us—holding us all
Together. Thick and thin. Hot and cold.
Credit and savings are so intertwined it's
Nearly impossible to tell them apart.
But here it is—spewed out across the page.

## Water
• • •

Thrift, Knowledge, Necessity. Water
Oozing through the basement floor.
Do you ever stop learning? Frustration
That is not pleasant. Solve the issue.
Water, basement, mold again. The
"French Drain" solved the water at
The base of the wall. Why, "French"—
This little ditch dug and filled with tiny
"Pea-sized" gravel. Perforated drainage

Tile (that means pipe) that catches water.
Invented of course. Everything is invented,
Discovered, slipped into consciousness
From some unnamed source—the
Silence of an idea. Henry Fowler "French"
In 1859 designed the system to drain
Excess water from his Massachusetts fields.

Do you care? Except it didn't solve your issue.
The mold growers put in the sump
Pump—it works until the first
Spring deluge. The hardest ever in
Your 40 years here—smashed into the
Side of the house—Torrents. Spring.
Welcome life renewal and WATER—
More than Mr. French's invention could
Handle. The mold growers-uh-remediators
Want to tear out the entire floor—more
Pea-gravel, more drains, more concrete.

## Hurry UP
• • •

Thrift sets in. They're nuts. A small
Fortune already, and it's still not so bad
All this mold and moisture—*damn*—
Dizziness, frustration, but you're
Out of it. Just put our house back
Together. We'll deal with it. Engineers
Hold the world together and these are
Not the ones—ignorance at a good
Price. A curtain drain—but not
These guys. Enough is enough. Good
Sense takes over—frustration—good

Sense, and a solution with people,
Workers you know this time. A deep
Trench on the uphill side—gravel, pipe
Lead the precious water away from
Your house. The foundation. They've
Done their job to the extent of their
Knowledge. They're paid—Hurry up.
Move on. Upstairs into the light and health.
You're thinking clearly now. Old Age—
Yes. But knowledge says—get it done.
Get out. Thank you for your services.
There comes a time. And thank you
Mr. French, but it wasn't enough. Don't
Dwell on it. Knowledge, good health, net
Worth and engineers. There's always
A solution somewhere in there—in
The silence where ideas flow freely—like
Water—water channeled into a "Curtain Drain."

## Loving Service for Others
• • •

"Loving Service for others," was the term
Dropped by the mothers around the table
Last night for the 20th birthday of a grandson.
It was their way of recognizing the energy
That goes into preparing a meal—indeed
Any activity by any member of the family
That smooths the life of the household and
Each other. Imagine the chores—teenager,
Emptying the trash, washing the dishes, cleaning
Your own room, and maybe even other
Parts of the house—life changes from "I don't
Want to"—to "Yes, of course." Loving service

For others—Imagine that, you oldster—
As you make the journey back into your shell.
Stay alive. Stay involved. "Loving service
For others"—Can there be anything more
Health-giving, engaging, fun, even—than
Emptying the cat box, bagging the trash,
Delivering it to its receptacle—shopping,
Cooking, making a living, making a birthday
Cake for anyone—than "Loving Service
For others." What a switch in attitude it
Can be. Drudgery is reduced to Zero.
On the assembly line, behind the teller box,
At the desk, dreaming up the next song,
The next project. It's all about me—
You mean—others—you mean us—you
Mean society at work when you look at it
This way. Thank you, Mothers. Dads agree!

## Remembering
• • •

Remembering can be a hazard or a joy.
Children playing jacks on a roof top—flat
Surface—skipping about—in India. The old
Woman's smile as you round the corner in the
Alley. Just smiling—through a few missing teeth.
The playground adventures in grammar school.
Struggles always for dominance and self-worth
With your peers until you settled it with threats
And fists and you found your place in the
Playground hierarchy. But you didn't stay there.
All of you moved on. But the dynamic didn't.
Holding hands—a kiss and exploration. It all
Seemed so worthwhile and settled you down

To whom you were. The big city—a gun to your
Head—fury and violation—acceptance. Here take
The $35, and is it any different today for
An entire country, except they're fighting back.
You didn't know how—you long-haired
Hippy. You left it all on the playground.
Today it's discussion and short hair—
Deals and seeing that as many people as
Possible get what they want—you're influential,
Now—or were. There's joy in remembering.
There's joy in Results, which you can still
See—the families, the people, the roles.
The concrete poured. Society in action.
You remember. You can see it. There's pride
There is humility. Remembering for you is more joy
Than Hazard. Loving Service for others. It works!

## Jury Duty
• • •

Driving a friend. That's the plan—to see
His 90-year-old dad—who is also a friend.
You pack—not much—it's only overnight.
Back the next day to basement, Curtain
Drains, and the big clean up. Jury Duty
Looms. The big clean up—Society in action.
Protection, equality, the LAW. You called
As required—number 202 on a list of 225—
It's not likely you'll have to go. The one
You love had to go—a dozen years ago.
Called to the Court House in our nearby
Village. Silence every night. No discussion.
Sequestered some nights. Serious. Silence.
And later—4 children and a wife disposed

Of in a fire—arson of their farmhouse
In the country. Too gruesome to think about—
Hear about. As the man left with his new
Girlfriend—do these things really happen?
And was arrested bragging in a bar—
Life in prison—the jury— *"GUILTY"*—
It did happen. On the jury of 12—you
Had to hear about it. And a bond developed
Between them, among them—and friendships.

And today—not often, but sometimes,
Driving together on a back country road
You hear about it—that was the site.
That grassy knoll—where the house was—
Demolished like the lives within it.
Could it really have happened? And a year later
A summons came for jury duty. The One you love
called in as required. "Report
On Monday," and burst into tears. The clerk
On the line asked what happened, and
Was told—" Don't worry. You'll never
Have to serve again." Compassion at last,
From the Courts. Across the world—

## Across the World
• • •

No law, no compassion, as missiles
Continue to drop. Wives and children
Murdered in the fire. Why does it happen?
Why? …*One man's distorted opinion of himself.*
Too gruesome to think about—hear about.
*GUILTY* in the court of the local village.
*GUILTY* in the court of the civilized world.

## An Elderly…
• • •

Drive your friend. Friendships…
Hold the world together. "Loving Service"—
For a friend. And is there anything more
Bolstering, healing, and fun, taking a visit
To a Father—an elderly father—four hours away.
Our elderly is a mother—90 years old
And steps away in the cottage behind the house.
Safe, secure, walking her dog through the woods.
Daily—snow or rain—sun, wind, it makes
No difference—7 healthy children with families
Not so far away. Meals—once—twice a day
With us in our kitchen. Movies by the fire
Bring the dog. Scrabble, Quilting, Sewing. Driving
Still—a healthy, happy, active life—we all visit
And share. Those dogs! Freedom is a wonderful thing.

## Freedom
• • •

Manure too luscious not to roll in—
Spread on the fields around the woods.
And they're off. Oh, for leashes—too
Late…you wait. Come back to the house.
You wait. No dogs. Your Love takes the
SUV—neighbors—no dogs. Back home.
You both wait. Meanwhile the neighbors
Who often call—you call—No, they
Are not here. We'll call when they show
Up. So you take the old, red, 160,000
Miles SUV—the "Dog Car""—down the
Drive, along the lake. Past the houses.
Past the cottages. Turn—a mile up

The hill to the State Highway. They never
Go this far. Turn left—another mile
In the traffic—our country "blocks"
Are one mile square—left over from the
Military Tracts divided up across the
State and given to the Continental
Soldiers as payment—640 acres—1 mile
By one mile—State highway—halfway to
The next turn down to the lake. You see
Traffic, Flashing lights, six cars, a tractor
Trailer with hazard lights and two of the 3
Brown Ones—as big as ever—as smelly as
Ever—ambling among the cars and
Across the road—so glad to see you!

## Smelly
• • •

Smelly—you open the back. They jump
In onto the towels and blankets so
Smelly and so happy. Your love pulls
Up across the road—lights still
Flashing—the girl in the black
Car calls out—she has the 3rd
One. And instead of going to the car
Of your Love—pulled up on the
Other side—the traffic is getting restless,
Creeping—the darn dog walks across
The State Highway as you stop everyone
Again. Ambling, so happy to see you,
So happy to see the Red Car—you
Open the back hatch, and in she goes.
Three smelly—at the moment— *"bad words."*
You love them, you just love them

You can't hate them. They're back!
The neighbors had called—several
In the square mile that is compressed
Between the lake and the State Highway
And the woods and manure laden fields.
It's Spring—what do you expect!
They've never—never come this far.
Never run this far from home—
What is this about Freedom Abused?
But it's Spring!! Abused. And now life
On a leash—as much as you hate it,
As much as they hate it, will be the
New norm for a while. Sometimes
Boundaries are necessary. And baths!

## Life is Good
. . .

No leashes inside the house—just cozy
Comfortable blankets to curl on, as
They watch and accept the invariable
Pats—scratch this, yes under the chin—
Roll over, and it's the belly. They're a
Few gray hairs forming around the
Muzzle now. But life is good. No
Guilt here—just purging and rebuilding.
Would that you could send this peace
And comfort across the world—and you
Rely on Silence and the deepest of
Meditations to carry the healing to every
Spirit at their depths—even across the world.

## Uncivilized
• • •

Silence, purge, regrowth. May it come to you.
Enough. Enough. Enough. A curative trip
Won't help this one. You've gone already—
Cairo—you and your love were there
The day of the invasion. You didn't even
Know. You'd been kissing camels in Giza—
Kissing on camels. Pyramids in the
Background—stability, longevity, total
Fun. And the Nile. 5000 years of the Nile
Valley—its tombs excavated from History.
The sand covered it all, and you thought
Civilized began just over 2000 years ago.
Not so. We're hardly "civilized" even today.
It's a tragedy—an uncivilized tragedy
Across the world.

## A New Start
• • •

Covid, Cancer, and Cardiac problems
Become rampant as we age—even as
Relative youngsters. When the trips to
The labs—to the doctors—show you the
Right numbers—and you have survived—
In good health now—it's *Life Afresh*
In your body now, as well as just in
"Your mind."—A new start—a continuation
Of a "Normal Life."—if there is such a thing.
The greatest challenges now are more
Than getting out of bed, dressing,
Going downstairs. They expand back to
Normal—the trips—the deals—who

Can you help besides just yourself—
And with what. Friendships return
For they are two-way—more than a
Cripple and a caregiver. Vitality. Let's
Go somewhere! The engine's running—
80 miles per hour is a sure thing now.
Let's get out of here. But here is good too.
It's secure. Your arms around those
You love—at least once a day. Heart to heart—
Always. She makes the meals. He makes the
Meals—She makes the plans. He makes the
Plans—happen. Or He and He—She and She—
It's the bond—the affection—that ties
You all together. Friend to Friend—Love to
Love. You have the right numbers now, and
They are good!!

## Reset
. . .

"Special Savings!"—which huckster is after
You now? You carry your link to the
World in your pocket. And just like the
World, it comes to you in all forms—
Truth, untruth. Love, affection, and
You filter out the things you hate. And
Hate is the word for the trash and junk—
Those invasions, unwanted, uncalled
For in your life, which you carry in your
Pocket, and you can choose to ignore it—
If you can put up with the vibrations
And the ding-dings—Someone's after you.
Reset.  Maybe you'll run out of charge
Someday. But you keep plugging the darn

Thing in. You choose to stay connected
To "life as we know it." Turn it off for a
While. Pick up one of those old-fashioned
Things you have suckled your news from
All your life—the smooth shiny paper,
The dull white and black paper. You
Want your desires to be your own—self-
Generated—truly yours. And even here
You're shaped and formed in a strange
Deceitful way—Buy this. Buy that—more
Sex—it's all yours—the ads without the
Ding-ding and vibration. The hucksters
Have it. The liars have it. Buy this
And stuff it up your desire machine.
You'll feel better—guaranteed!

## Purpose of Life
• • •

We are not meant to suffer. Why do
We continue to do so? Unfulfilled
Desires—but whose desires—the hucksters?
Turn in—inward—deeply in and to
Silence. There you know—in the
Quiet—the pure quiet and intelligence—
The Consciousness that is yours—Yes,
The Purpose of Life is the Expansion of
Happiness. You can trust that. It's not
Carried in your pocket. It's carried
At your core—that soul that is
Enlivened in the Silence and permeates
Every cell and fiber of the You.

## Efficient Action
• • •

This you can trust. It explodes in
The light you find—lingering, quivering,
Poised for action, as you emerge from
Silence—knowing what you want.
(And it's not that ding-ding in your
Pocket!) and you are ready to
Function in the world. And you know
Where you are going—Duty, Dharma, Desires
All blend into strong efficient
Action—no matter what your age—
No matter how fast (or slow) you drive.
You can run with your walking stick—
Go down the stairs backwards if you have to—
But it's yours. Your own speed. Your own
Vision—and you know what to do. You
Don't need "Special Savings!" you've
Got it all already—at your core.

## Mutual Interdependence
• • •

Bone of my bone. Flesh of my flesh.
It aches when you're not here. What's the
Matter? Have you lost independence?
You might say—but close your eyes
And you feel the dependency—the inter-
Dependency—the merging of 40 years together.
It's OK. You can manage. You want the
Best for each other. But you can't deny
The ache. Growth, love, separation
Have indeed merged together in mutual
Interdependence that permits long periods on

Your own. Each of you—independent at your
Core—the Silence together. It's OK.
All OK. There are no bombs dropping here.
You're together in your aloneness. Exploring
Experiencing, always the silence of Pure
Consciousness. Believe it, for you're living it.

## Heart to Heart
• • •

It's time to get back to work—the
Projects, the lists that sustain you, tie
You to Society, friends, and each other
Even when you're parted. Flesh and bone—
Heart to Heart—that expands and covers
The distance between you. For there is
No distance when your fingers hold the
Fingers of your loved one even across the
World you're together. The is no ache
Between you. The ache is only in the little
You that shrinks with inattention until
You return with will power and alacrity to
*Life Afresh*, and you know the other is
There—here or not, they are there—for you
They are there. Believe it. You know it's true.
In ten days they'll be home. In ten years?
That's unknown and you've always
Had unknowns. We grow up with unknowns,
And we embrace, as they ever emerge
And become knowns—assembled into
Youth—the middle years—old age, and
This new period—*Life Afresh*. There
Will always be unknowns and the bone
And flesh of another always make it

Bearable—even though you know
You're strong and could do it by
Yourself if you had to. But you don't
Because the other is always there
Even in separation and silence—
Heart to heart—so work hard and rest
Peacefully. And get ready for the next
Trip together—Duty, dharma, desires, all
Blend into action whether you're alone
Or joyfully together.

## Anticipation
• • •

Sold out. Your names are on the plaque
Over the lobby doors which for two years
Have been closed—dark. Two years—no
Joy, no comedy, no music—Oh—Deep Star—
Dark, which nearly blew your head off—
Packed then, but only recently. 1600
Seats of bustle—soft roar and squirming,
Moving into your assigned row—the hum
Of anticipation. First row for you. Flanked
By two 90-year old's you have brought
For a little jolt—you're not quite sure
What—only that it will be lively and on
Stage slightly above eye level for you—
Looking up with anticipation and memory
Of the ever-changing possibilities that
Have exuded from this state—this
Collegiate Gothic hodge-podge of arches,
Glitter, gold, and blue—curtains of
Sound that surround, as you wait
Flanked by 90 years of life and glory exuding

From the stage—and you, only slightly
Younger. Full of anticipation with
The thrill of the crowd. Hearing aids—In.
Smiles. Snacks—thank you…Waiting…

## Poised for Action
• • •

Four chairs, microphones, wires, stands,
Speakers, lights—a red cello—covered
In plaid gold prints and lines to your right.
Coming toward you—a skin covered
Djembe drum—goblet percussion—West
African decent— *"djembe"*—maybe
This is it— *"Anke dje, ankebe"* translate—
"Everyone gathers together in peace."
At least that's why you're here.
A tiny red electric keyboard perpendicular
To the front of the stage—nearly in
Your lap—one musician it appears
Will play both instruments. Next chair—
A basic drum set, cymbals, snare, and bass.
The fourth chair—accordion and tiny
Concertina. All basic. All poised for action.

## Ukrainian!
• • •

The yellow fuzzy full-stage backdrop
Reads— "No War—No Putin" in blue
Fuzzy drawings. We're ready—
No program. No explanation. And out
They walk. One man. Three women. The women
Wear Cossack tall black oily sheepskin
Hats—the man—maybe a scarf—Ukrainian!

How can they be here? 6 weeks ago
Was the invasion—the war of hell—
You assume they were already here and
Your producer was able to book them—
*DakhaBrakha*. It means "Give and Take."

## Sold Out
• • •
So appropriate—a Folk Music Melee
Explodes on you—piercing, wailing,
Beating and sliding into rhythms
Complex and beautiful—No war. Stop Putin.
Dissipated behind them into abstract haunting
Faces parading across the screen—
Jolting, wailing. Too much—front
Row speaker twenty feet from your
Head. Hearing aids out! Ear Plugs
In. Raucous, cacophony changes to
Bearable beauty—your pair of 90-
Year old's sit in enjoyment and for an
Hour and a half we're taken through
Abstractions of sound and visuals—
Romping across the screen—tearing into
Our heads—non-stop—keening, rhythm,
Whistling, bird, and nature sounds all
From the four of them—their voices, their
Heart into our ears—non-stop keening,
Rhythm, and images of war all before
Us on the stage and the screen—
"Give and Take"—Ukrainian—
*DakhaBrakha*—look them up. Oh my God—
Help us all that such beauty of sound
And imagery should pierce us to the core.

That peace, love, and restitution
Should all return to their country—
Our country—Sold Out! Give and Take!
*DakhaBrakha*—a world away—a world here.

1600 people on their feet—yelling and
Bellowing for two more encores…
Original—? This was it. Sold Out!
No war! No Putin! One world!
*Life Afresh!!* Even at 90 years old!

## Growth
• • •

What really matters? Focusing your life—
Your energy towards growth. At your
Age? Yes, at your age. What's the
Alternative? Don't worry. It's going to
Happen. You don't have to disappear in
Moldy self-pity—no matter how bad it gets.
There's life, and joy, and growth to be
Had—and lived. You gave up nearly, in
Memory-loss, dizziness, and Covid. Even
Your 90-year-old friend, who walks with
Two canes and eats sardines and yogurt
For lunch—keeps going—mind sharp
And useful running his business still
At 90—gathering about him the loyalty
Of 35-year workers still forging ahead.

## Discipline
• • •

You have the discipline to continue.
Don't kid yourself that you don't.

*Life Afresh* is a decision. It's theatre.
It's money. It's sharing. It's trips.
It's hugs and pats from the one you
Love. The ones you love—all of
Them. It's discussion. It's problem
Solving. Put that wisdom to work.
Enviable in all that you have
Brought to Society—those around you.
All of us—Advancing the Cause! —Continually
In our own way. Slopping about in
Indirection is a waste of time, a waste
Of life! That precious commodity—5000
Years old and preserved in jars and
Tombs for when you come back!
You're not a Pharaoh—you don't need
That—as fascinating as it was—Egypt.
Bombs you don't need, or fires, to
Enforce your will. Persuasion and
Listening work just fine. All on board
Get what they want—or nearly so.
"Give and Take"—Wailing and Keening
Into the future. That's what matters!

## Spacious Dreams
• • •

Spacious dreams—Roaming the world.
Deflecting negativity. Absorbing
The positive—the friendships and
Deluge of good thoughts that seep
Through the mesh of your memory.
It's slipping—you can't deny, but
Acres of grass and fields and
Wildlife revitalizing with bird songs

Sunlight and Spring in full bloom
Have their effect and counter the
Occasional slip off the rails—the
Hiccup of where did you put that—
And what is supposed to happen next?

Taking on tasks keeps you vital
And keen and sharp—the mind steps
Up with the right words, the right
Direction for the immediate—it's
Yesterday that gets a little foggy
And that guy's name you were just
Working with. But the thrust—the direction
Is good. It's solid and can be trusted—
To unfold the solution. You know.
And the nightly dreams zoom you
Into a reality that bathes you in
Comfort and satisfied desire. You
Adjust to the one away being gone.
You anticipate their return through
The occasional ache in your heart…

## A Moving Sea
• • •

They will be back—and only in a
Matter of sunlight and a few days
Of torrential spring rain. Strength,
Positivity—ensue from remembering
That fact. So much is getting done
In their absence—mold cleaned. Kitchen
Painted. All set in motion before
They left. Divide and conquer is
A concept that has roared around

You both embroiling you both—
Together and apart in solutions—
Productivity— 'make not a bond of
Love—let it rather be a moving sea
Between the shores of your souls…'
You remember that. You both live
That through nearly 40 years of
Being together—married. What a
Blessing to humankind to have that as
A concept as marriages intertwine us—
Bone of my bone—flesh of my flesh.

Dreams bolster. Actions satisfy.
Memory inadequate. Take all you want.
It's on the house! The one you have
Restored, rebuilt as one would a
Broken marriage, guided by desire,
Happiness, friendships, and knowing
Your life and grounds were meant for
Sharing world-wide—your guests.
And you remember the Prophet—
You live his words—both together.

## Commitment
. . .

You're tired. That's not a reason to quit.
It's a reason to rest. But you can't rest,
Not now. You're committed. Committed
To friendship, promises made, responsibilities
Accepted. Commitment overcomes rest.
Commitment overcomes quitting. Give up
On commitment and you give up on who
You are. It's a deep interior form of

Energy. It shapes and forms a meaningless
Blob of clay. It's self-generated
Because you're alive and want to
Accomplish. It regenerates in the silence
Deep within you which is where you
Go for rest—in balance with the
Activity—and the activity takes shape
From commitment to an idea, a desire,
A promise—even a list you decide on
Of the projects to be done. Pushing through
To completion. Confusion can block your
Way. Settle down. Put things in order.
Direction will become apparent. The projects
Are there. You know them. Advancing
The cause—of beauty, friendship,
Helpfulness, 'loving service to others.'
Keep them in mind. Energy returns.
Rest comes naturally without dropping
Out. No quitting. You summon the energy,
And the need to rest passes—regenerates
Into that thing that needs to be done.

## Will Power
• • •

Will power—we're made of it—at our
Very core—we can summon it—like
Shackleton attempting to cross Antarctica.
We can Survive. Nearly dead—we can
Survive on will power. Obedience—
To whom? Ourselves. Societies' norms—
Trusting in what we want and going
For it. That trip sounds awfully nice.
But there are some things here we

Need to take care of first. Then we can
Go. Figure out the solution—No
Giving up here. It's fun to eat
Well. It sustains you—maybe too well.

Scales? —Drop away from your
Eyes—but don't lie about your
Body. You'll survive—even a little
More of you than you might like. It's
All wrapped up in moving forward—
Getting that job done—meeting your
Deadline, doing what you committed
To do—to yourself, your friends, to
The one you love. You're not tired
Any longer. You forge ahead with
Energy. Tired was—is—a state of
Mind. Sleep deeply when you sleep.
Work hard and focused, you're
Awake. "Tired" will no longer be an issue.

## Your Father
• • •

Patience—interesting world. Your father
Was not one for patience—worked hard he did.
Patient he was. Patient actually
On an interior level—building boats, airplanes
Which he flew, employees he supported
And made sure they were paid before
Himself. Weekly trips to the church with
Mother—in all that, he was patient.
Military patience. Get it done! Here's
Help if you need it. Here's freedom to
Go it on your own (and make mistakes) if

You need that. Here's how you fit the
Boards together, paint properly—with the
Grain. It's time to learn to shave—believe
It or not. Growing up in his image for
He's your father—and the impatience,
The lack of patience is—looking back—
More with you—attempting to live in
Perfection that with Father's influence
Became the standard until you broke
At 31 and gave it up in disaster and
Unwilled incompetence. Patience crumbled.

## Patience
• • •

Looking back—after the rebuild— it's
Apparent now decades later what strength—
Sinuous physical and mental strength
Emanate from the patience—that stability
Forgiving yourself—so quickly and quietly
In the instance of turmoil, indecision,
Lurking evil, lurking temptation. Patience
In the instance, to reorient and go the
Way of growth, gratitude, loyalty—
And forgiveness—even of yourself. It's
A "second look"—the breath you gulp—
And change direction—or follow the
Direction you intended to take all along.

Patience and Silence go hand in hand—
Strengthening, you like the touch and
Fingers of the one you love holding you
Steady. It is self-generated. Regenerated.
Stopping, breathing, looking ahead—

Forecasting the next move and doing
It—making it because you were
Patient—soaking up the strength of
That second look and knowing outcomes
Would be OK! OK and health-giving
Versus crumbling and wrinkling into
Smell-laden oblivion—brokenness.
Patience, prayer, internal reorientation.
Do we actually understand patience?
Self-generated composure opening
The window to a sun-filled world
Of Will-Power, productivity, and fun.
Without it, fingers cross, steps stumble,
Anxiety reigns. With it smooth
Flowing openness guides our activity
To complete satisfaction. —Patience—
Live it!

## The Birds
• • •

Strut. Your large white parrot
Struts across the floor and extends
Her foot for you to pick her up
And replace her in her cage. Her
Crest rises. She screams—not in defiance
But because she is a Cockatoo—three or four
Pounds of bird with a beak that
Can smash an almond shell.

Strutting intimidates the dogs—they
Steer clear. That beak, that strutting
Aggression is a little too much for their
Gentle outlook on life. The African

Grey—peeks out of her cage— 'I see
You. I love you!' Her cover is over her
For the night—huge cages six feet tall—covered.
She peeks out, and you know she means it.
Such affection bred through 20 years
Together. And with another 60 years
To go—you'd better plan on a super-long
Life—or make out a will. Who wants
These birds? Cage cleaning daily.
Huge 25 lb. bags of food every
Month. And don't forget the
Hispaniola Amazon—green, blue,
Red—and the White Faced
Parakeet, who is totally green.
It doesn't get any better than this.
And mention the outside birds—40 lb.
Bags of seed every week—for their
Six feeders—and the squirrels.

## The Zoo

• • •

We keep them around for our dogs
To chase. It's all important. The
Garage for three cars is, as your cousin's
Wife from Brazil called it—a Zoo!
"I didn't know you had a
Zooo—" she accented to us on a
Visit so many years ago. We tried
Keeping a car in the garage the first
Night with the dogs—40 years ago,
And they ate the cowling off the
Front of the new Saab—so it's now
Our "Zooo...." Heated, scruffy old

Carpet and four sofas—Spring and
Fall—the huge move—everything
Out—sofas, cages, carpet, in the driveway.
Hose down the concrete floor and
Start again—such contentment
On everyone's face. The birds
Sing. The dogs grin and stretch out.
Life's normal here.

## Ambassadors
• • •

You heard on NPR
From Boston today that *DakhaBrakha* wasn't
Already here when the invasion started—
They were sent out as Ukrainian
Ambassadors—the day after the invasion
To garner support from the World.
Daily now—you peek out and say—
"I love you…." It's all so strange.

## The Moon
• • •

The moon—hot and round awakens you
Through the blinds, centered in the
Mullions of your upstairs window.
You arise—open the slats for a full
View—a lop-sided orange orb descending
Ever so slowly into the tree tops bare
Of leaves—a tangled web of sticks
Begins to obscure its view. At 5:00 AM
This is so much better than the basement!
You watch. You watch. And it's gone…
A brief moment and lucky you—you

Just happened to catch it—revitalized
At 5:00 AM.

## A Painful Drama
• • •

And your love called from town—
Huge ache in her tummy—should you
Drive to town and get her? No, she'll
Make it home. Should you take her to the
Hospital—No—No hospital! She'll drive
Herself—slowly—but it hurts. She's weak—
She tells you. A take-out dinner in the
Car—shrimp and soup. Then two hours at
The Gem Roundtable where an ancient expert
Sits at the head—a dozen (mostly ladies)
You've been—and it's so expensive—
Surrounded by Diamonds, gold, and
Glitz—true glitz from the mountains
Of Peru—the caves and mountains
Of Oregon, the ancient lady knows them
All—turquoise is a small seam in
The rock—gold, new seams—secrets are
Being found all the time—and emeralds—
The good ones—the deep green rough
Rocks—karats thick, are no longer being
Found. A dozen ladies (sometimes men)—you've
Bought—and it's a thrill—for this wedding,
That Christmas gift. Bought and later mounted
By the jeweler—a dear friend for decades—
So well skilled—renown—

But the tummy ache became too much.
She leaves. Calls you. Drives home—stamina as always

# LIFE AFRESH

Despite the pain, At home to bed! A
Soaking bath in the garden tub prepared
As she enters—bath salts—a bath—still
Hurts—and to bed—nightgown ready—and to bed.

It hurts to experience her hurt. You
Know. You've been here before—a caress
A foot rub. You'll be down the hall—you
Assure her. You leave. She cries out—
You return—You leave again—half
A dozen times you patter back and forth
As she cries out…Tea? No tea. Water?
Yes, water—the spring water bottle you
Open and give to her as she raises herself
To accept it—drinks—and flops back down.

The futon on the floor becomes your
Bed as you rise up to help her—
At each groan of pain. It's serious,
And finally she settles down. You sleep
On the floors and minutes—lots of minutes
Later, she awakens—pain again. What
Is this! What did you eat! Shrimp…

But she's OK now you patter back down
The hall. An hour later you awaken.
Her light is on. Quickly you return.
She's indisposed—and you see and hear
The results. So much better now.
You open her upstairs door to the deck—
Fresh spring air enters. She cleans
Herself up. You assist—and she lies
Down—relieved for the moment. You

Stay and then return to your room. Such
Pain she has had. Your phone! Look it up.

Quickly. "Food Poisoning"—Symptoms
Causes, cures—and yes— "Shrimp—
Shell-fish—mishandled—a bacteria—huge
Ache in the stomach—nausea—the 'd' word,
The 'v' word—she's got it all as she
Expels whatever it was—and it may
Last a few hours—even a few days—phones
Don't lie. Most likely she'll be OK,
No hospital. Wholeness, peace
And sleep return. And you patter down
The hall to sleep until the moon
For its instant—peeks through the
Blinds—which you open and for an
Instant—enjoy the beauty at 5:00 AM.

## Misdiagnosis
• • •

Take control. The pills—supposed to shed
Pounds—are a joke. You listened to the
Promises. You ate your sugar covered
Donuts as they promised you could—the
Svelte bodies on the huckster's screen. Always,
At least for you—it comes down to dropping
Sugar—more exercise. You're disappointed.
Money-back guarantee—so send back
The pills. With yourself, off the scales. It's
Hard to admit—you lost nothing but
Your dignity and self-control. Take
Control—relive the past two days—

The pain did not subside down the hall.

Sleep came but sporadic. The pain shifted,
Or did you just not remember—left side—
You thought—but now—right side
Lower abdomen. Same symptoms as
Food poisoning—continuing. Lower right.
Of course—it takes a while to sink in—
Yes—Appendicitis—Your love agrees
Between winces—Ambulance!
Gurney—the trip from the country to
The hospital. Do you want the slow
Ride—the EMT's ask—or the fast
Ride—No bumps please. Don't wait.

If you don't get to town and buy the
$5.00 per gallon gas—the invasion price
You won't be going anywhere. You do,
They do—and you meet them unloaded
At the hospital—Masks. ER.

## Surgery
• • •

You know it well—the hundred-people-
Bustle—admitted—cared for—nurses
Techs. Stretchers and rooms—constant
Maneuvering. Constant calls. It's silent
In her room—#5. The drip. The gown. The
Antibiotic peaceful—pain controlled.
Lower abdomen. You sit and talk and wait.
The smile emerges—the relief. Going for a
CAT scan to confirm. You wait alone.
Eyes closed in relief yourself. They
Rolled her out on the hospital bed.
You've been there. In good hands.

Peaceful relief is building. Return. Doctor.
Surgery. When? Tonight. Wait. Wait. Wait.
Down the hall they roll her. You patter
Along beside, dodging the crushed,
The broken—the I-can't-take-it- anymore
Groans and hurts as you pass the
Curtained bays, and thank God for
Hospitals, and nurses, doctors, and
Stretchers—rollers. It's grown from
2:00 Ambulance. 3:00 Admittance—
To 10:00 at night. The anesthetist—dark blue
Except for his masked face. Allergies?
Name? Food? Not since yesterday's
"Food poisoning"—you'd called the restaurant—
Shrimp.... Now you'd have to call them
Back—not Shrimp—Sorry. Appendicitis.
Your shrimp is OK. My mistake—
Same symptoms though. The surgeon arrives.

Your love is wheeled away. They
Send you to the waiting room. You can't
Read the Bible—The print's too miniscule.
Your glasses are at home. Forgotten. What else?
You wait. In what seems like a few minutes—
You were prepared for an hour or more—
The surgeon is back. "She's fine!" She'll be
Here overnight—come see her now—and you do.
A groggy smile up from the hospital bed—
Laparoscopic—hardly an incision—a smile, a touch,
A kiss. The pain is gone. Amazing. Amazing.
Tomorrow come back and see her as early
As you want—the doctor says—as early—

40 years together. That matters. And she's
All right now. That matters even more.

## The Morning Visit
• • •

Giving care—intense attention and care
Becomes a joy once you get past the
Receptionist—"Visiting hours don't start.
Until 3:00." It's 9:00 AM. "You'll have to
Wait." The doctor said last night—come
Anytime—you can see her. "Visiting
Hours don't start until 3:00" Listen Lady,
My wife had emergency surgery at
11:00 last night…at 3:00 PM I can see her?

Seldom Does anger arise. Nine years on the board
Of the hospital…I know where things are.
You can call security. I'm going
Upstairs! You don't strut. But nearly so—
You stride past to the elevator—
Third floor. No one notices you when you
Walk with intensity—cleaning the halls
Taking care of the patients—you're
Ignored and you find her. It's 9:30 AM
She's sitting up—smiling as you enter.
Her breakfast tray is the only thing
Between you. You sit. She's fine.
She's fine and relieved you're here.

## Humanity
• • •

This could have been so much worse—
A trip. A boat. The mountains—Ladakh—

Where the two of you have often
Talked of going—Nepal—the timing
(Between trips—at home) couldn't
Have been better—if it had to happen.
Serendipity. A black shirt with Security flashes,
Pauses, and then leaves the doorway—
A man can visit his wife—there's humanity
Beyond the rules. You don't often barge—
But you did, and you're here with the
One you love—whole and fulfilled
After last night's—yesterday's scare,
And Security will not interfere.

## Peace Offering
• • •

Hospital menus—you help her fill
Them out—Lunch, Dinner, Breakfast
Again—how long? The nurse said
Do it. You do it. You talk. You wait
Together. And wait. You both agree.
Banking is important. You need to go.
You leave the room.
It will be a while, a day, half day,
Two days—neither of you know—only
Recovery—that's the important thing
Now—Down the elevator. Past gurneys,
Patients. More bustle—past the
Cafeteria. Stop in. Maybe she'll like
Butterscotch pudding—a sealed container
In the refrigerated section—a spoon—
Pay—and striding gently up to
The receptionist's station, you place
Butterscotch pudding on her counter—

She looks up— "Peace Offering," you
Say. "My apologies for Barging Past."
She smiles up at you, and it's all OK.

## Pain Relief
• • •

Healing—another world, whether you walk
In off the street, or are delivered in an
Ambulance. A 4-day later reflection.
What's love got to do with it? You
Quiver with love as you listen—Morphine—
It felt so good—the instant they connected
The tubes in the ER and it flowed.
Sympathy—pain relief—renewed well-being
It would be so easy to become addicted
That miraculous Poppy plant—the source
Of Opium—and 200 years ago you
Read—synthesized into morphine—less
Addictive but so effective in pain relief
Allowing surgery without pain
Flooding one with relief, love, well-being
Why do these caregivers, nurses, aides,
Surgeons, come in off the street to
This profession? Self-love, as they pour
Themselves into their profession. Dignity,
Pain relief, expertise, and health returning
To all of us who have been under their
Care. Morphine—it can't be denied is
A rush. And thank God it was controlled
And only for a day your love said.
A chemical and pharmaceutical
Wonder—the steps to bring you down
And release you with a pill—

"Up to four a day"—Hydrocodone also addictive
And after a day—your love stops—it
Feels "too good." You've had friends,
You've helped others through addiction—
You look out for yourself through
Experience, self-love, knowledge, and
Switch to Tylenol—non-addictive but
Not as effective—but the pain becomes
Bearable as you heal—bearable
As you swing your legs over—you're
There to help and watch the winces

## Healing
. . .

And the Jackson Pratt suction drain—
A 50-year-old invention by two Naval
Surgeons fills the collapsed three inch
"Oval"—that comes a 'ball" taped to
Your belly, so the fluid from the incision
Is "sucked" down the tube—red with fluid.
You've read all this and watched as your love
Heals and shows/tells you the process.

It's a different world for you both
Off the street—even by ambulance.
You only go there when you have to.
Stretch a bit. Observe. Learn. Accept
The pain—the care, the love, the
Expertise that surrounds you in the
Hospital. It's not addiction—they know
What they're doing—and healing—
Return to Normalcy—is the end product
Of the Equation.

# Recover Yourself
• • •

Discipline—out the window. Does every
Day have to be a "good day?" Recover
Yourself. Patter down the hall. Your love is
Sound asleep. The winter storm in the middle
Of Spring did not materialize—no
seven inches of snow. What do they know…
The basement flooded again—the
System those idiots installed—
Nothing works. Return the pills—
They're worthless. Money finally
Went in the bank after two botched attempts.
Your dogs are quiet. No foxes screaming
In the woods to find a mate—the
"Vixen's Scream"—piercing cries that
Echo through the woods—delighting
The dogs to distraction as they bark
Their heads off in response—or maybe
It's fear. It's horrible—if you can
Call something of Nature's—horrible—
A sound. Suppose this was a "good day."
What would happen? Inner Silence
Is the place to recover. Your love is OK.
Just asleep. It's gray. It's misty.
The green grass spreads its way to the
Lake. It loves this weather—
Wet—borderline snow that didn't
Happen—the rain did. It's pouring
Up through your basement floor—probably.

# Plans Help
• • •

Plans help. The daily list—prepared the
Night before. And you're not even
Working—retired—to do what you want.
And for that—a list is just the thing.
A list has kept you together all your
Adult life—and it's still your adult
Life—that hasn't faded. The lists
Are as vital as ever. You walked
The land yesterday—a hundred acres.
Woods on a mountain top—a hilltop
Really—views across the valley.
Some dingbat set up a deer-stand
At the entrance to your trail. What to do?
Hunting is not in your scheme of things.
You ignore it and pick up the beer cans
Instead. Walking in, a half-mile deep
In the woods—an antique tractor, rusted
Into oblivion—early 1900's—huge steel
Wheels—a spark advance on the steering
Column—fender crooked and gone.
A tree fallen across the bare four-cylinder
Engine—all the color of a rusted vixen—
A deep, deep, rust to the point of beauty.
A treasure in its form with a hundred
Years of woods grown up on its
Once plowed land. Discipline's all right.
Someone had it years—a century ago. Let
It crowd back into your life. It's delightful here.
Get up… Move!

## A Strange Calm
• • •

And she's not moving.... Lying prone—covers
Surrounding her head. You watch for a
Moment. Stock still. Sound asleep, or…?
Sound asleep. No breath. You move closer.
And you can't hear well enough—is she…
Three inches from her face…still…she's still…
A strange
Calm. Let her…you move back toward
The end of the bed. Not panic—just
A strange calm. It's been painful and
Tough—this operation…so strange—this
Quiet and calm…no breath…no movement
Beneath the covers…And then—

## A Twitch
• • •

A twitch of the ankle, and you leave and go
Downstairs—still calm and curious about your
Reaction…to…nothing. And you cook
Her half-cup of soupy oatmeal—this sugarless
Staple she has thrived on for over a year
With Type 1 Diabetes. Your love has discipline.

Her doctor removed the tube from her tummy
Such relief and she's sleeping deeply
She appears at the kitchen door—smiling,
Very rested. And you say nothing about
This strange calm—only a 'glad to see you'
And a hug and kiss and 'eat your oatmeal.'
You bring the insulin pen from the refrigerator.
It's so easy to wait on the one you love.

You don't need chemistry to understand
The process. You just follow the steps—
The routine. And love the dickens out of her—
That's chemistry in itself. What more
Is there to understand? It keeps life
Going for you both. How could you
Have been so calm when you didn't know—
Whether…if…so calm. But the twitch reassured…
Life—a Twitch, and we're alive—
Free and active to go another day.
*"Life Afresh"*—Thank God.

## Hiding Under our Desks
• • •

What movie would the dogs like to see?
You look through "The Ten Best"—Lassie,
Incredible Journey, Old Yeller—no, how
About Beethoven? —Yes! And your
Livingroom Theatre—the screen as wide as
Two dogs—He's a Saint Bernard. Will they
Like it? A bark or two gets their attention.
Then they roll over and sleep through it.
Beethoven is a Saint Bernard. They're Labs—
Not much affinity no matter how adventuresome.
And Putin tested a new missile—at least
Threatening the West. From Russia. Don't
Mess with the man. The Bear, or you'll
Be "cyber-attacked and blown into nuclear
Smithereens. Your defenses won't see it
Coming." We're here again—hiding under
Our desks as we learned in third grade—
In case of Nuclear attack…My God, Our God.
Where are you? What's happening? Beethoven

On the run. Capturing the dog-nappers.
The children are finding the solution—
Speaking the truth. Catching the killers. Asserting
Themselves in spite of put downs and disbeliefs.
It's a children's movie after all. The
Children have to win. Our dogs are still
Sleeping—indifferent, on the floor around us.

## Who's Next
• • •

Crumpled Ukraine. Threatened Finland.
Worried Sweden—You lived there at 19.
For a year. Do they join NATO—confronting
Russia? Its leader who is insane with
Aggression. World War III looms. Does it?
No one would risk it. And the consequences.
 What would happen to your projects, your
Family, your net-nothing-ephemeral worth?
Exploded and suffering as is already happening
Across the world. Don't move or you're dead!
Just like on TV. One man has the drop on
Us all. His weapon—one big pistol with
A Nuclear Bomb on the barrel ready to fire.
We're helpless and all you can think about
Is a clean basement without mold—
And a healed love down the hall. A walk
In the woods. Normal life, and you're glued to the
Suffering. It's in your living room. It's in your
Phone—your ultimate source of late.
Did you see those tanks! Blown to pieces.
Buildings battered and gone. Bodies—Poor, hungry,
Yes, dead, people. How? Why? The bigger
Craftier sword wins. Gang up on the monster.

Do it world. Sanction him to death. He's not
Dropping his gun—just testing new missiles
In case you had doubts about his intentions.
It's a whole country under attack. Who's
Next? Russia is already the largest
Country in the world. Greatness
Is what he wants. To be the most
Feared? He's got it. A smudge—
He's attempting to add a postage stamp
To his holdings. And then who's next?
Over how many dead bodies?

## It's Their Nature
• • •

The Wind is blowing up a storm from outside.
Waves crashing on the beach. Two geese
Nested in the flower box on the dock—
Eggs—call off the dogs. Take them
Back to the house. Last year they
Destroyed the nest. Dogs do that.
It's their nature. The geese left.
Not this year. You'll protect them.
The dogs can swim elsewhere. Give this
Brooding life time to hatch without
Destruction. Here you can control
That. Do it. It's got nothing to do with
The ten best movies. Or Reviews,
It's just where you are. What you
Can control. Pay attention to the twitch.
It's reassuring—Life Continues.

## A New Beginning
• • •

It won't be long now. A day of tasks—
Reorganizing. Your 90-year-old guests
Will be coming tomorrow. Escaping the Covid
Outbreaks at their life-care facility.
They keep to themselves—but Spring by the
Lake—it's safe. Our house is safe.
Our pavilion—today we escape priorities—
The helter-skelter piling of stuff—
Stuff everywhere under the outdoor
Roof. It will be fun as we shake our-
Selves off and move into daffodils
and bluebells. Forsythia, and green,
Green everywhere—well-tended Grass.
It's a new beginning—as is every day on
This side of the world. We're not blown
To smithereens yet. We still briskly
Protect, and follow now our children
From aways away. And this week
Another trip. A plane. A boat. A
River—across the country. Snake & Columbia.

## Our Country
• • •

It's safe—Lewis & Clark. Our country
Grew too. We didn't bomb—there were
None. But we rode horses—covered
Ground. We terrorized expanded, and yes,
We killed. Gruesome and peaceful now.
Because of *POWER*—It's ours now.
We took it. Is it any different?
We can be outraged to watch it.

But it was done. And we look with pride
Now—most of us—on our Country our
Boundaries. We blew everything apart
To create it. Isn't that what's happening now—
Across the world. But no—we're civilized
Now. We have our parties—our get togethers,
Or did until Covid—until Ukraine—
Pause and caution. But life is exciting.
We're taking another trip—curative—
Yes. And Sunday brunch with friends—
All the more exciting because they
Are older—a window into the future
From an unrivaled past of fame
And accomplishment—Each of us in
Our small circle. Hang on for the ride.

## It Doesn't End
• • •

It will be a long one. Until it's not
Anymore. A future—Stretches us into
Oblivion. And by then it will be welcome—
A journey back into Silence—yes—
From whence we came. Your friend
Said there's nothing there—that's the
End. You don't agree. Today you'll paint
The shingles. Today you'll move the
Clutter. Today you'll organize vitality
For yourself and those you care about.
It doesn't end. The last breath will be a
Good One—Guaranteed! Enjoy today,
Tomorrow—beyond—have the friends over.
Take the trip…

## Order Will Prevail
• • •

Exhaustion. Sore in a good way. You
Hefted 200 lb. file cabinets across the
Floor—thigh and back muscles served
You well—a sofa—a ceiling-high
Bookcase—empty but a feat in itself,
Jockeying it into place against the wall.
The tile on the floor is a bit scuffed.
It will clean up. Sliding objects into
Place was the only option when you're
Just one—patient, skillful, like
Your father taught you—use your
Brain, not your brawn, but today—
Yesterday, it felt good—exhausting at the
Day's end—but to use both. Your basement
Is clean—not clean per se, but free
Of mold—that pernicious attacker of
Lungs and brain. It's taken months
But it feels like you outsmarted it—
Conquered it. You conquered it with
Patience, brain, brawn—and a lot
Of money. Green and moldy that changed
Hands in the long run—and it was long—
They probably knew what they were
Doing and soon order will prevail—
Order—Thanks—some more money—
And from here you'll do it yourself.

## Direct & Simple
• • •

One of your favorite things to do—
Establishing order—in space—yours

And others—In Life! Do it. Exhaustion
Can be and is overcome with rest, patience,
Muscle rub, and a good night's sleep
After a dinner, your love has prepared
And conversation. Your mother-in-law—
91-now—who fell and broke her glasses and is
None the worse for wear. She'll go on
This next trip—with a cane, new
Sneakers, and replaced glasses on Monday,
Direct and simple—we all create.
We all patch things back together.
Quilts are her thing—magnificently
Creative. The shingles you painted—
Cedar shakes with their soft reddish glow
Are now deep grayish-blue and ready
To be installed around the new entryway
Where she lives—the cottage behind—
With her Irish dog, her cat, her Sewing
Machines—four of them—and
Her quilts. 91 years old and an
Inspiration—broken glasses and all.
Independence—We all have a modicum
Of it—at our core. It keeps us going.
Interdependence—with that
We can thrive, not selfishly, but with
The support of friends, family—the
World around us. Advice—take it.
Exhaustion—overcome it. You know how
And have…

## The Thrill of the Ride
• • •

Shared values—a friend showed up in

# LIFE AFRESH

The late afternoon. You heard the soft
Putter of his motorcycle—Opened the
Shade—he waved. Out you went. Red—
Bright red—British, from your childhood,
Or at least your adolescence. Looking
Back is so much fun. You admire it—
The friend too. Your age… Business
Associate in town—retired. Your bike
Sits in the barn—also British, but black
And cream. You sit in the rocking chairs—
Appropriate—under the roof of the Outdoor
Kitchen. No fire in the fireplace. It's warm.

Spring. And reminisce—Do you remember
The…And that deal—your friend
Was the attorney. He never "sold out," but
He finally sold his properties.
His wife rides too—the back roads of the
State—the rivers, hills, mountains
Avoiding the Interstate Highways—Why?
For the pure thrill of being alive!
Not as steady…You concur…But the
"Bike" commands balance, respect,
Cleaning, care, and upkeep. It takes you
Into a space of balance, adoration
Of just living! And your time will come
After the basement, after the next trip.
Spring in full bloom. Maybe you'll ride
Together—burning up nothing but the road—
And Old Age—It's gone in the curves,
The acceleration—the balance. Always
The balance—like sailing, flying, living
Your life. You turn it on with awareness

Churning through the weeds of indecision
Of problems with others—the harmony—
You just keep balance and ride right
On through. You're still doing it. Both
Of you in your way—your expertise.
Joined together for a few moments
In memory and the thrill of the
Road, the thrill of the deal—the thrill
Of overcoming all blockages, and you
Reminisce—two—say it—"geezers"
On the porch—in their rocking chairs.
Overcoming old age—together. *Life Afresh*.

You take a few pictures—him by his bike.
You'll send them to him later. And you
Return to where you were—the other side
Of the shade—inside deep in the Silence
That you return to with the one you
Love at this time of day—sunset—
Silence. Balance. Meditation—every
Day for nearly 50 years. It won't be
Long. Shared values—balance. Silence.
Motorcycles and thrills—accomplishments.
And they're blended together in "The Thrill of the
Ride!"

## Your Curative Trip
• • •

Running away on a River Boat. The
*American Pride*—superficial paddle wheel
But reminiscent of olden days—
Oregon, Washington. On the Columbia.
Lewis and Clark—1805—their journey

# LIFE AFRESH

Opening up a way to the West. Hardships
For 17 months. Thirty-six men—
Canoes, rapids, Native Americans—
The US Army—sent by Jefferson.
Another curative trip—100 people—gray
Hairs, blue hairs, no hairs—fly in from across the
Country into Portland. Board the ship. The crew
Handles the luggage. Your "curative trip"
Idea is truly catching, as you cast off
Downriver 100 miles to Astoria where the
Columbia joins the Pacific at "Cape Disappointment."
Which is not a disappointment—a
Lighthouse, a submerged sand bar
And a 'thousand ships' strewn across
The bottom of this unruly merging
Of river and ocean that has intrigued
Sailors and explorers since the 1600's,
And sunk their boats. It's safer today
As you dock this floating Elder Care
Facility—fake paddle wheel and all
In this town named in 1810 when
John Jacob Astor (of NYC) sent his
Newly founded fur trading company
To the West Coast—hence the name
Astoria—and a bus carries you down
Safely across the bridge to explore
The park and hike the trail a mile
Down and up—a true "Breather," if you
Still can. But it's worth it—the view
From the pinnacle—the view with history.
And one of the world's wealthiest
Men at the time—furs—opium trade
And Manhattan real estate. He died

In 1848 and his son who became the
World's wealthiest man sank on the
Titanic in 1912. Not that we talk
About that on our trip. This is all Lewis
And Clark and opening up the West.

## This is Fancy
• • •

Museums and lectures. Full dining room
Teaming with servers and more than a
Normal menu. This is fancy. Salmon and
The Manhattan Project. Top secret in
Harden, Oregon—50,000 people.
Workers, scientists refining Plutonium
For the end of World War II and the Bomb—
Hiroshima—and the continued threat
Today—daily in the news, across the
World—Atomic Energy—World War III
And the end of life as we know it.

And it's all floating up the river
With us as we turn and traverse
Nine dams—locks that raise our little
Ship 740'—along with the few
Salmon that can make it up the fish
Ladders—to spawn and less than
One percent do—and they are dying. Tear
Down the dams—for the sake of the
River, the sake of life. It's being
Considered. The sacred wheat from the
Midwest can go by truck and train
To China—the many barges won't be
Needed. If we're all still here.

Which you realize of course we
Won't be as you thread your way
Among the wheelchairs and walkers
Deck to deck, elevators and private
Staterooms on this end-of-life
Floating-Dream-Boat.

## Look Forward
• • •

Where is the next trip?
It's planned—With the kids
The next generation. Get out of here.
Costa Rica will do—surfing, zip-lining
Hikes in the rain forest. Youth and the
Future surround our family
Gatherings that you take annually
Except for the Covid years. Alaska,
Yellowstone, Lake Placid, Newport
Virginia Beach, Key West. It's all good.
Get off this boat. The History was History.
We're all history soon enough—Look Forward!

## Weight & Exercise
• • •

The Cardiologist—you see him once
A year—no, twice. Blood pressure, EKG,
All fine. No lumps. No bumps. You're
Healthy—no pain. Two heart attacks—nine stents
Over, was it ten years? Whatever it was,
You're OK. Do you exercise? Not much.
And your weight—You need to lose
Some. Don't they always say that? Yes.
But he's right. He tells you—weight and

Exercise are the two things you can
Control—they will improve your health.
They will improve your quality of life.
He's trim, fit, himself—he lives the drill.
And you know the drill. You drive away
In your fancy car. Come back in a year,
He has said. So you know you must be
Better—better over time. Weight and exercise.

## Sugar
• • •

And it's sugar—You know it's sugar.
You are addicted. And it is an addiction—
Like your friend on Oxycodone—You're
Not swatting nurses with your back
Scratcher—but you are addicted. How
Many times have you tried (and failed)
To break the cycle. It feels so good the
Nibbling rush from the between-meal
Cakes and cookies—the chips and the
Snacks. Your weight and exercise—
You know it—solve it!!

## S-S-A-E
• • •

A new mantra—that may help. Think
This every time you reach for that
Cookie—the between-meal rush to
The top of the heap—think this—
S-S-A-E. *"Stop Sugar And Exercise"*—
Do it! And for 3 days now you've
Endured the pain—the creaking agony
Of the no less than 20 minutes

(Longer is better—a good pace is better—)
Walk with the dogs. You don't have to
Trot along with them through your woods,
But you can be brisk about it.
And have an apple—fruit—natural
Sugar—not refined—it doesn't fly
You high. It is not addictive. And
You know from the many times you've
Tried—weight drops away—after
The painful week you settle in
Until the next binge. But maybe this
Time…try it—you know it will
Help—to keep you around—even with
A creaky heart. S-S-A-E—it's so—
Terse—so easy to remember—a reminder
To Self-Control. You will it. It will
Happen—like everything else you have
Willed, explored, and obtained in your
Life. What do "I" want? It works!
Better health. Endurance—Fun S-S-A-E

## Once Again
• • •

It's working—four days now—you feel it's
Working, but you steer clear of the scales—
A few pounds off and Bam! —You're
Back on the sugar binges—so just keep
S-S-A-E in mind—and let it go. No scales to
Give you the false sense of it's OK now—
Just a little sugar. That's the way it goes
With an addiction—just one drink—
Just one pill—this time it will be OK
Your body tells itself—but it won't be.

In a day you're back on the high—
And it's happened so many times over
The years. You function. We all eat
Sugar—love sugar—but it's only, at
Least for you—the objective realization
That it is insidious. It will reach
Back out and grab you, and the weight
Will soar once again. You miss the
Buzz—but not the achy joints—the
Internal inflammation—the arthritis
That seems to creep in as you rub your
Knuckles to relieve the ache—that's
Gone with the sugar. You're not a
Dietician, only old and experienced.
So try it once again, only this time
With your new mantra—that stretch
Of short sounds so effective and easy
To remember—S-S-A-E—*Stop Eating Sugar And Exercise.*

## Nothing…Nothing
### • • •

So what's wrong then? It's always an
Adjustment—Physical Malaise as you
"Withdraw." But something else is floundering
Around in your brain and body. You attended
A huge event locally last weekend. Your
Son was honored for a land donation he
Made to a civic group. A friend came up
And complemented you on how much your
Family continues to do to support the community.
You modestly thanked him—and it felt good
Of course, as he mentioned this thing…that

Thing… you had done, and your wife, and your
Son. It all felt good and you thanked him
All the while looking at his cap and dark face—
Smooth—even though your age. It ended.
You smiled, nodded, and walked to your car.
Something bothering you, your wife said?
Oh nothing…nothing…—his name. It's
As familiar as your own, but it wouldn't
Come. It didn't surface. It's so disturbing.
She gave you his name, and you laughed,
And relaxed—somewhat—but it bugged
You. Lack of food? No. Lack of sleep?
No. Lack of memory—you realize…
It's just a fact. Nothing to do with sugar.
More with senility. And you hate it.

## Relax
• • •

So find your props. Jar your memory
With your notebooks, your semi-organized
Scraps of paper—Your lists… Your lists.
You've always used them. Self-generated
Organization, Self-generated Insights…

What do you want? Write it down—
Now especially—now that you need it.
And if something doesn't come to you—
Relax. It will. In time it will—
Until it doesn't. And your significant
Other—the one you love more than
Yourself—the one you live for, would
Die for, give your life for—Support
Her as she goes through her ailments.

It's that time of life—Ailments—
The body doesn't "just happen"
Anymore. You realize. Like the
Leaky, moldy house you've just
Repaired. Darn if there wasn't water
In the basement yesterday—and
Water in the kitchen ceiling—a
Broken pipe. More trouble. A
Leaky roof—it comes in spades.
Accept it. Don't accept it—Fix it.
Repair it. Get in the help you
Need—Plumbers, Carpenters, Electricians,
Surgeons, Doctors, and friends for the
Motorcycle ride. You leave soon for the
Next trip? Stay right here supporting each other.
For the Next Trip. And in the meantime—
Make your lists.

## Still Here
• •

It's growing dim. Soar right out of this
Mire. You've done it before. Friends—absorb
Their vibes—in silence, if necessary. Stroke
The cats, pet the dogs. Smile in Silence
If that's what it takes to regain your
Equanimity. And then the talking comes—
Spontaneously. You're not broken. You're
Not an idiot. Take it as it comes. Make
Your lists. You've always made it happen—
Reengagement with life, your friends,
Yourself, and those you love. Another
Trip—you just had one—moderation.
At home is where your attention, your

Your energy needs to go. Rest as you need to.
Listen—Process. You're still here. There
Are things to do. Remember your pills—
After several days without them (you
Lost the carefully sorted pill box)—
You realize, feel the effects, the
Sluggishness—heart, respiratory, memory—
All these combinations that keep you
Alive and functioning in reality. You're
Still here.

## Give and Take
• • •

You sailed. Maine—Ocean.
Winds so strong you shuddered, but
Took them in stride—over 50 knots
X 1.2 = 60 mph—and in a boat—
Your large boat and with friends—you've
Sunk your resources and energy into.
And yes—it was scary—but only for
A moment—as you furled, reefed—
Adapted your boat, and life to the
Conditions. Nothing unusual. Keep doing
Just that—*Life Afresh*. It's OK to
Stretch out now and again. It wasn't
An explosion—it was, as always gradual
Adaptation. The news however was an
Explosion. So many children—Texas—
Shot dead in their school—and Ukraine
Being crushed in their resilience. So much
Evil in the world as you deal with
Winds of howling, steady fury, and you
Adapt. Even at sea, cell phones keep

You integrated with the issues—the
News, the friends, and family at home,
Around the world. And the conversation
With a friend taking you back into the
History of your lives. The so important
Exploits, achievements—those things you
Can brag about with a friend who
Appreciates evermore getting to know you
And sharing the entangled aspects of
Their life as well. Give and take—
A slight push to the ridiculous, as like
Two kids you bond in your revelations.
And life is good, sharing it with a
Friend. Now find those pills and continue on.

## This Life Business
• • •

Friends and Family. You remember them.
They will remember you, at least a
Generation of them will remember you.
That's not so important. This life business
Is a private endeavor at its core. Once
You've found, explored, developed, and
Lived it—dependent—as you are on
Those around you—those who shaped
You, you realized—fully developed,
That you exist as a pulsing act of
Self-generation. And it is in this mass of
Energy, ideas, and feeling that you meet
Those you love, those you interact with
And do business with, generate new life
Create the kids and mutual endeavors
That spare nothing to shape the world

Around you all. The ALL of you—so many
Who have come—gone—shared their energy.

## Their Names
• • •

Think of their names. You'll hold them
That way—in your arms—in your heart—
Your own private place at your core—
Those who loved, supported, drew you
Out so you could go safely in—to
Self-realization without going mad—as in
"Stark-raving." They kept you safe until
You were ready. They shared the growth—
The results—the joy and energy of
A life well-lived with you, and you with them.
Think of their names. These are your
People too—the forces they represent
In everyone's life—those whose lives
You touched and whose lives touched yours.

## The "Address Book of your Life"
• • •

Each of us has our own list of names
Representing some major or minor portion
Of ourselves—in this private
Endeavor that has developed into our
Life—Mother, Daddy—No, not
Roles—*NAMES*—each one lives in our
History—our memory, in a unique,
Unspoken way—silent, as we remember them.

Walter, Bissell, Guy, and Mary. Phebe, Elsa,
Each name—a person—their own energy

Now in some way embedded in you.
Betsy, Frost, George, and Bill. Wanda, Bob,
Judy and Jean. They all had roles—but
Now they are names—Roland, Dolly,
Skip and Norma. Ron and Carrie, Thys,
Alan—so many Alan's—Rick, Charlie, Terry,
Scott, Katie, Carol, Sally, keep going—
Many more—Nancy, Robbie, Della, Gabe.
David, Jeff, Chris, and Ben. Alicia, Alice,
Beverly and Locke. Martha, Simone, Arthur.
Tracy, Tom. Curt—

Who are your names
Those who have touched you shallow or
Deeply—Names—Karen, Allyson, Chuck,
And Matt. Barbara, Sven, Harold,
And Christina. Jacques. Per-Johan,
Bertil, Inga—others so far away
Across the Sea—of your life.

Bitte, Lynn, Beth, Meg, and Susan.
Sandy, Mike, and Dewey. Each name
A memory—a small or large splash
Of memory, influence perhaps, but influence
In that they touched you. Doug and Dan,
Dale, Mariann, Tony, Barb, and Neil.
Ryan, John. Blasts from the past and
They are with you. Julian, Melissa, Ruth,
Erin and Hali. Old, young. They are with you.

Miles, Abi, Wellsley, and Sidney—whole
Families of names. Lloyd and Gigi. Shari,
Frank, Wendy, Larry—close and far away.

# LIFE AFRESH

Each one a smidgeon in your soul.
Each name a life of energy and history
Interwoven into your own. Gary, Lisa, Marilyn
And Cal. Glenda, Abe, and Denise. Who would
You invite to your party? Who are your
Names? Eric, Ken, Knox, Gray, Connie
And Prudence. Margo, Joe, Micah, Mandy.
Paula, Grace, Kirk, River, Stone. Livy.
The party grows—Perry, Richie, Sunita, Anthony.
Lila, Brad, Monica, Linda, Pam and Ross.
Barry, Ruthye, Heather, Bruce, and Jim—

They'll all come to this party in the ether.
Neva, Jon, Synnove, Alf, Harriet, Nikki,
Jeremy, Tristan, Brigid, and Teddy, Brittany
Evan and Finn, Dallas, Travis. Close
And far in time and space. They are your
Names—a fraction of behind the scenes
Of your life. And there are scores more.

You'll never list them all, but they are in
Your heart—Emelia, Anders, Ed, Tricia.
Cara, Quincy, Forrest, and Dean. Marty,
Maggie, Elaine, Dorrit, Kathi, and Carl—the
Address book of your life—old age, and
Life Afresh. It won't go on forever here.

And through this maze of before and
After—wherever it leads—it will be
Courage, Confidence, and Gratitude,
That guide you:

*Courage to face your greatest challenges.*

*Confidence in your abilities, whatever
They are, to move forward— "Advancing
The Cause."*

*Gratitude for the spark—the energy of life
Given to you since conception, and the
Opportunity to put it to use shaping
Your own life and the lives of others.*

Courage, Confidence, and Gratitude—they matter.
These and your list of names that bind you in a
Passionate Embrace—

to—
***LIFE'S FORCE***

# BACK COVER PHOTO

· · ·

Washing an Elephant in Thrissur, Kerala, India 2014
Photo by Tony Sorhaindo

Elephants are considered Symbols of Peace, Mental Strength, and Power—Wisdom, Courage, Longevity, and Patience. They are known for their memory and care of their young and members of their herd. "Lord Ganesh" the Elephant God is a symbol of perfect wisdom and revered as the "Remover of Obstacles."

# ACKNOWLEDGMENTS

• • •

My thanks to the mentors and friends who have assisted me in surviving this far! They are many, but include my parents, Bissell and Phebe Travis, my sister Wendy, my wife, Carol, former wife, Synnove, children Elsa and Frost, my niece, Wellsley and family, and good friends, Carl, Meg, Tony, and Tony, and Ron Leifer—all people dear to me. For a more complete list see the final pages of my book! I also thank my business partners and friends Tom Seaman & Norm Dykema and Stu Lewis, a mentor for years

And thank you to the production team that has assisted me through yet another book—Della Mancuso, for her editorial and production experience. Donna Murphy for the design and layout. Dear friend and artist, Lynn Keller, who traveled with us to India and painted the exquisite watercolor "Washing my Elephant", used on our cover. DSB who read the manuscript, and Tony Sorhaindo who also read and commented. And to MMY who half a century ago breathed new life into a broken body and spirit.

It is those we gather around us who make our lives interesting, happy, and productive.

# ABOUT THE AUTHOR

...

A business mentor to family and friends, at 80 years old, author Mack Travis can look back on a 50-year career in real estate development, civic engagement, and avid ocean sailing. He and his wife, Carol, still keep a hand in the family business, but they also keep a 42-ft classic wooden yawl in Rockport, Maine, where they have sailed summers for the past 25 years.

*Surviving Old Age* is Mack's fourth book since his retirement from the family Real Estate Development and Management business. Other works include:

*Creating an Independent Income in Real Estate*, 2011; Second Edition 2020

*The Expansion of Happiness—A Common Sense Look at Transcendental Meditation*, 2014

His career summary—*Shaping a City, Ithaca, New York—A Developer's Perspective* 2018—is the story of how he and many other developers and community members formed a Business Improvement District, developed three 10-year strategic plans, and transformed Ithaca from a sleepy upstate New York town, into one of the "Best Small Cities" in the country.